EX LIBRIS
TSM

Patrick O'Donovan:
A JOURNALIST'S
ODYSSEY

Patrick O'Donovan brought great distinction to whatever he wrote. I always read his work with interest and admiration.

Basil Hume
ARCHBISHOP OF WESTMINSTER

Patrick O'Donovan:
A JOURNALIST'S ODYSSEY

*With a personal recollection by Robert Kee
and biographical notes by Hermione O'Donovan*

Esmonde Publishing Limited

Published in Great Britain by
Esmonde Publishing Limited
31 Tonsley Hill, London SW18 1BE

Designer: Richard Kelly

Set in Bembo by TJB Photosetting Ltd., South Witham, Lincolnshire
Printed by Nene Litho and bound by Woolnough Bookbinding
both of Irthlingborough, Northamptonshire.

*I should like to thank all those who have helped in the production
of this book but none more than David Astor without whom it would
not have been possible.* H.M.O'D

British Library Cataloguing in Publication Data

O'Donovan, Patrick
    Patrick O'Donovan: a journalist's odyssey.
    I. Title   II. Kee, Robert   III. O'Donovan, Hermione
    082   PR6029.D5/

ISBN 0-946680-11-6

CONTENTS

MR. PATRICK O'DONOVAN

Mr. Patrick O'Donovan, the author and journalist, for many years on the staff of *The Observer*, died on December 23. Educated at Ampleforth and Christ Church, Oxford, where he read law and was elected treasurer of the Union, he served in the Irish Guards in the Second World War and was demobilized with the rank of major. He then joined the staff of *The Observer* and travelled widely for that paper winning golden opinions, particularly in the United States where his interpretation of the affairs and ethos of America won him several awards. His inclinations and style were admirably suited to the big occasion and his reporting of grand papal events brought him much praise. But he was versatile also, as his dispatches from the war in Korea made plain.

Mr. David Astor writes: Patrick O'Donovan, *The Observer's* special correspondent in the post-war decade, was a descriptive writer of outstanding talent. He had an eye for places as well as people and an instinct for the meaning of events. As a young foreign correspondent, he recognized as a positive force the tidal-wave quality of Mao's revolutionary war sweeping through Canton when others were treating it as just another shambles. At the other end of his register, he could describe formal occasions such as a state funeral, or prosaic events like a school sports day or even the Boat Race (which he reported from the streets of Hammersmith) in a way that both amused and moved. In style and

humour, he had an affinity with the poet John Betjeman and his written words, like Betjeman's, always seemed intended to be read aloud. His scripts for broadcasting did not need to be read by an actor to be dramatic.

Patrick came of a strict Roman Catholic family of the professional class, and he never renounced his family's faith and disciplines. But he also had a baroque taste for the extravagant gesture and occasional touches of Gaelic abandon. Managing these contrary inclinations called for all his intelligence and underlying seriousness. His talent for self-mockery also helped. It was, however, these inner tensions and his unexpected shyness that probably helped him understand the tensions in others. Nobody less keyed-up could have interpreted the feelings of both Arabs and Jews in the early days of Israel with such directness.

The course of his life took a decisive turn when, quite early in his public career, he made an inspired marriage that committed him to all that he held most private. In his last years, living at Alresford, he cultivated his domestic circle and read history and architecture as if he were a student. He wrote two monographs of great figures of his beloved church, one famous and one almost unknown. Yet he never lost his amused curiosity in people and the passing scene, which was ultimately what made his personality and his writings so attractive.

The Times, December 1981

7

'A quality of vividness...'
A personal recollection
by Robert Kee

Patrick and I became friends in youth and heard the chimes at midnight up to a point. He liked – and I was always flattered that he did so – to welcome me as his 'oldest friend', by no means strictly true because we had first met at Oxford in the late 1930s. Largely through my own indolence, we saw each other less and less over the past two decades, but he would still greet me like this whenever we did meet and I was always amazingly pleased, though with typical elegance he would manage to place an increasing touch of comic ambiguity on the syllable 'old –' as the years passed. But there was something about his personality that gave true substance to the notion which otherwise, alas, might have become just more and more of a joke. There was about him a quality of vividness which not only entered everything he wrote but endured timelessly in the minds of his friends so that even if one had not seen him for a long time it was always as if one had only just seen him a few days before. It is still like that now. Possibly everyone sees this quality in their friends. I am just saying that it was in him in the same measure as it was in his journalism, which is as alive today as when it was written, sometimes over thirty years ago. Anyone who reads the pieces in this book about the end of the Kuomintang or Palestine in 1947 or the Korean War can see this for themselves.

My memory of time spent with him at Oxford and in London just before and just after the outbreak of the war is of a slightly arrogant, amusing, generous and educative friend, whose Catholicism gave him an ordered structure from which to view fairly effortlessly the world and its many ordered interesting facets. In this respect I was both less sure of myself and less well-informed than he was, and as a result both grateful to him and, I see from looking at an old diary, also rather envious of him, as for instance when he was able to insist that the low-roofed Lady Chapel behind the altar in Southwark Cathedral which a notice called a 'retro-choir' was not in fact a retro-choir at all.

Diary entries made at the age of 20 can reveal the writer's own shortcomings more than anything else, but I quote the following passage because I think it shows the first traces of the journalist he was to become in the making.

21st December 1939. Patrick came over twice last term from Sand-hurst. It had done him an awful lot of good, purged him of what some-times used to be too great a preoccupation with his own effect on people, and given him a wider sensibility. No, this is wrong. It is his preoccupation with his effect on people that is his greatest charm. This is as strong as ever, but now never too strong. Whereas he used only to be interested in other people when he was a success he now combines this with being interested in other people for their own sakes. It is this attitude of sociable selfishness that makes him so charming and more effective.

Possibly the diarist's mood had been affected by noting that 'his Oscar Wilde locks have been cut off and he looks like a very young bird that has left the nest prematurely, his new hairy tweed suit adding to the effect with a first-vestige-of-feathers look.' But I think it was the ability, spotted burgeoning here, most successfully to blend a theatrical effect with a human approach to people and events that was to be the secret of both his personal and his journalistic style. It seemed delightfully appropriate in a painful sort of way to hear after the war that the wound he had received in Normandy had resulted from his standing up dramatically in the turret of his tank to encourage his men and be struck on the chin by a concealed German road wire.

The hairy suit, incidentally, had been made for him by an Irish Guards tailor once situated in Maddox Street to whom he introduced me after the war. 'A very nice gentleman Mr. O'Donovan is,' said the tailor filleting with his tape measure. But when I reported this back to Patrick he expostulated: 'Gentleman! I'm the grandson of an Irish peasant!' His joyous ability to have his social status both ways was equally an ingredient in his success.

From such happy resolution of his own paradoxes came

doubtless his gift for focussing in words with such dazzling definition. Both in his personal relations and in his journalistic style he would sometimes affect what at first sight could seem pomposity in order in a most devastating way to deflate pomposity and display the truth in a sort of glory one would not otherwise have sensed. Through his writing, millions of people he never knew must have been able to experience the same warmth, vivid insight and sense of fun that was the reward of his friends.

In his hey-day he was fond of self-deprecating badinage about the relative statuses of 'journalism' and 'writing'. Because 'writers' wrote books and not to a deadline he maintained that they cossetted an inner sense of superiority and he would proudly declare himself 'just a reporter' with the same pseudo-humility as he would proclaim himself a peasant. I am sorry to have to tell him, now that he is no longer there to protest, that those who read this book find themselves in the unquestionable presence of a writer of power and skill. And since I cannot help feeling that I do somehow hear him protest that his sort of journalism is old-fashioned anyway, now, I cannot help answering back – Patrick, art thou sleeping there below? – that in an age in which television, either by simply presenting events or else by interminably analysing them for us, deprives our imagination of the power to apprehend them, his sort of journalism is needed more seriously than ever.

Part One

BIOGRAPHICAL NOTE 1918–1967

Patrick O'Donovan was born, the first child of Dr. W. J. O'Donovan and Ethel Kate Kempton Smith, in Richmond, Surrey, on 13 June 1918, and was baptised a few days later into the Catholic church. His grandfather, encouraged by the headmaster of his native village of Ardfield near Clonakilty, in West Cork, had won an All England scholarship which brought him to Essex to take up a job in Customs and Excise and he married an English Methodist. Dr. O'Donovan was their eldest son. Brilliant, hard working, ambitious and dedicated to his Faith and despite the sometimes irresponsible and wayward behaviour of his wife, Dr. O'Donovan became a leading Harley Street specialist and for a short time Conservative MP for Mile End. His behaviour to his family was Victorian; his wife's unpredictable. Patrick was their only son. He was sent to Ampleforth to be educated by the Benedictines whom he loved, went from there to Christ Church, Oxford and on the outbreak of the Second World War he joined the Irish Guards.

After the war Patrick could not face the prospect of returning to Christ Church to complete his legal studies, and· through his two closest Oxford friends, Robert Kee and Nicholas Henderson, and the percipience of David Astor, he joined the staff of *The Observer*. His mother wept: 'You *cannot* be a seedy journalist.' For the most part, he sat about in the office library trying to adapt to the change in his social and financial status – Irish Guards major with hundreds of men in his care to office boy. On *Observer* writing paper, in July 1946, he wrote to his English master at Ampleforth, Dom Columba Carey-Elwes, O.S.B.: 'Dear Father Columba, After a few very unsettling weeks I have landed a job as a journalist here. The pay is exiguous and my position could hardly be more humble. I get about 6 pounds a week and they call me an apprentice. They tell me it is a good paper to start on and it looks as if I shall soon be sent to report on the fringes of the Iron Curtain. .... It is very different from being an elderly Major in the Irish Guards, but no doubt I shall get used to it. I have only been at it a couple of days and seem to have spent most of the time sitting in a large leather chair in the library. ....' Frank Pakenham (now Earl of Longford) intervened. 'Either you pay and employ this man properly,' he told David Astor, 'or you sack him.'

In December of 1946 newsprint was still hard to come by and under various pseudonyms the small staff covered every aspect of the news in carefully trimmed reports. Then, one day when the office was practically empty – even the agricultural correspondent, in some other guise, had been sent abroad to cover a story – Patrick was sent to Berlin to visit the Army of Occupation. It was the beginning of his long and very full career as a foreign correspondent. In all he reported on eight wars, in Greece, Palestine, China, Indonesia, Malaya, Korea, the Congo and then the Six Day War in 1967. He used to remind doctors and priests ruefully that he had certainly seen more dead bodies than they had had hot dinners. When in England he lived in Marylebone, his 'village', and delighted in all the English places and customs he had remembered with longing when abroad.

In 1950 the African continent was emerging as a place of change and unrest and Patrick was sent for a year to report. It was still the time of great Chiefs and occasional colonial splendours. In Buganda the Kabaka's Chiefs and Elders knelt to him and his people prostrated themselves at a respectful distance touching their cheeks to the dust. Tshekedi Khama in Bechuanaland was Regent for his nephew Seretse who broke the rules by marrying Ruth Williams in London – and got away with it. Kenyans went in terror from the Mau Mau; General Smuts was buried in Pretoria. Having had published one book, *For Fear of Weeping*, on his earlier tour of the Far East and China, this time Patrick put aside the idea of writing one on Africa. Things were changing too fast and he had orders to go to Korea. Anyway, he did not believe in the value of books by reporters. Their writing he considered ephemeral and destined only to line drawers and wrap fish and chips.

In 1954 the Queen made a tour of her Commonwealth. Patrick, without regret, left Korea and moved on to New Zealand and Australia. He fell in love with Australia and for a time dreamt of editing a newspaper there. But he had never led an office life and it would not have suited.

Unexpectedly called home in June 1954 to his father's deathbed, he married, and the following year was sent to replace Alastair Buchan as permanent correspondent in Washington. Over the next five years he twice won the David E. Bright Award presented by the University of California for the best reporting on America by a member of the foreign press. Georgetown replaced Marylebone as his 'village' and he made the most of a not particularly exciting time in American history. Truman had gone and J. F. Kennedy was still only a Senator who could not be persuaded to call him anything but Pat. He witnessed the launching of America's first spacecraft; from the United Nations he reported the debacle that was Suez and agonised over *The Observer's* controversial role in the crisis; he followed the inevitable pre-presidential election trail and celebrated the statehood of Alaska. He lectured endlessly on Britain, and with his wife, fulfilled the semi-diplomatic role of a British foreign correspondent.

Back in England in 1960 he became a home-based roving correspondent. At a moment's notice he flew from crisis to crisis: an earthquake in Chile (wearing a marvellously opulent and wholly unsuitable fur-lined coat lent for the outing by the Editor) and another one in Sicily; floods in Italy and Portugal; the horror of the war in the Congo from which one correspondent returned so shocked that for a time he suffered from amnesia; the Six Day War in the Middle East.

After England, Israel, Ireland and Poland became his 'other homelands'. In Poland he found the historical similarities to Ireland comfortingly familiar and it was the only Communist-controlled state he found tolerable. Jerusalem he loved as dearly as his Hampshire home, and knew as well. Ireland he visited as often as he was offered the chance. He did not believe in holidays, too much of his time was spent from home in any case, but opportunities arose quite frequently and his particular delight was to visit Clonakilty and the minute village of Ardfield from which his grandfather had come. They ensured his affection by making him Man of the Year for West Cork in 1966, an occasion as hilarious as any he had ever enjoyed.

But in 1967, while reporting on floods in Portugal he became ill and immediately on his return had the first of the many operations (thirteen in all) that haunted him for the rest of his life. Although it was almost inevitable that the strain of travelling would make him ill (the flight alone was an ordeal, twice he had been in a 'plane that had had to make a crash landing – 'If God had meant me to fly he'd have given me wings'), he continued to do it, but came home again and again to return immediately to hospital. From Gallipoli, from Moscow, from America....

Special Correspondent

Guarding the shrines

Jerusalem... On Christmas Eve it will be the last time that British authorities will guard the celebrations of the Birth of Christ. For the last time it will be a British soldiery that clumps through the vast Basilica of the Nativity down into the stifling cave. At midnight the clangour of the bell, announcing again one piece of news that has never lost its savour, will rock across a country rent in two and constrained for the last time by British law. There will be little peace and no goodwill. The very road to Bethlehem is now a place for violence. No Jew may use it unless he is armed or escorted. Others fear to use it lest they be mistaken for Jews, for it is a road which leads to Jewish settlements, passing through Arab lands. Recently a Jewish convoy was ambushed there, and its pathetic escort of Jewish settlement police were butchered as they left their open truck to get into a ditch. As a result, Bethlehem is all but deserted. The great worn Basilica seems as empty as a railway station at dawn. There is an old beggar woman at the back forever on the verge of tears as she creeps on hands and knees through the dust and whines for pilgrims that no longer come.

Arab touts who will show you the birthplace of Christ for a few shillings are desperate for customers. They pluck at the rare visitors and follow them through the great empty aisles and down the twisting staircase into the Grotto of the Nativity.

There, in the light of innumerable lamps in a glitter of silver and gold, the air heavy with incense and mystery, they press their grimy cards and assure the visitor that their souvenirs are the cheapest and the best. Upstairs in the Basilica they still chant the liturgies through the empty afternoons. I was there the other day, the only visitor. Before the gold iconostasis three women moved from ikon to ikon, bowing and crossing and kissing. They wore high linen wimples, a fashion that the

15

crusaders left to the women of Bethlehem. A few Greek priests, whose Christmas is not till January 6th, and who control the altar and choir of the Basilica, harshly shouted Psalms across the empty spaces as if they were exchanging insults.

Alongside, in the Latin Church, which is as ugly as only an Irish parish church can be, Franciscan friars murdered vespers behind the altar of their dark, deserted church. For one night at least this will be changed. Some of the bustle will return and the church will again be filled, though not as in former years. For now there are fewer soldiers and many people will not dare the trip to and from Bethlehem in the dark.

The District Commissioner of Jerusalem, neutral and neat in white colonial uniform, legal descendant of the Roman proconsuls, will be attending for the last time. Ever since Britain assumed the mandate it has been his task to maintain what is probably the most elaborate protocol in the world. He maintains a strictly defined *status quo* among the different communities who keep their sacred embassies at the holy places in somewhat unedifying rivalry. As a member of a faith that claims none of these things, he maintains for others the exact ownership of every hanging lamp, the exact position of every scrap of carpet, the exact rights which each may have to the hanging of a picture, the sweeping of a stair, or the route of a procession. It will be his task to see that no brawls occur in the Cave of the Nativity when the Latins go down to pray.

In the past the various communities, Greeks, Latins, Copts, Syrians, Armenians, and Abyssinians have all in turn complained of his rulings. Now they are viewing his imminent departure with considerable alarm. None of them has any idea what will replace his authority. Many of them are of Arab stock and wonder how long they will be allowed to maintain their neutrality. To a lesser degree these Christian communities engulfed in a turbulent sea of Arabs and Jews are sharing the strain and forebodings of the country. In the Old City of Jerusalem their shrines are disturbed. In the great Armenian convent of St. James the tiny cupboard rooms that surround its courtyards are filled beyond belief with nervous Christians who have fled their homes in the city to avoid the troubles. In the little Syrian convent on the site of the house of St. Mark they have crowded into the sacristy, are sleeping on cope chests and under vaulted arcades. They have set up little homes with grotesque red ottomans and bundles of bedding and all the dingy confusion that displaced persons everywhere create.

Only in one place have I seen complete normality. Up on the roof of the Holy Sepulchre there exists a small sad community of Abyssinian monks. Slowly and inevitably through the ages, with no great power to insist on their rights, they were edged out of the great church and now they live precariously among the fanlights and domes. Their cells are holes in the wall, fragments of older cloisters crudely patched with boxwood and corrugated iron. I saw one of them sitting with his back against the little dome that rises above the Chapel of the Finding of the Cross. He wore a heavy black habit; he also wore a Balaclava helmet and brown army gym shoes. Motionless, he was staring into a little manuscript book, reading painfully and holding the book a few inches from his eyes. Such detachment is not easy in the Holy Land. Even the Trappists in their silence at Latroun must look down on a concentration camp for Jewish extremists.

As in other years, sweet English carols will be sung in the Byzantine Church; Latin prelates will move through their ritual; Greeks will watch jealously that no ancient right be usurped; soldiers will kneel, though this time with rifles between their hands and clips of ammunition in their pockets. There has been a semblance of order this week if not of peace. On Wednesday night there will be many praying that the following Christmas, when the mandate has been surrendered to the United Nations, may be at least as quiet.

The Observer, 20 December 1947

The British leave

Haifa... When General MacMillan stepped aboard his launch in Haifa harbour he was the last British soldier to quit Palestine. He waved to the British Consul, standing a little lonely on the Jewish quay and holding under his arm the flag they had just pulled down. The launch sped across the crowded harbour, breaking across 31 years of British administration in Palestine. The General did not look back. A few minutes before he had stood with his ADC and a naval officer alone on a small square of the quayside that was still British. A single Marine bugler sounded a fanfare and salute and the flag came running down from the masthead above the Port Authority's office. A stiff breeze opened it out at the last minute and flung it sideways in a wide, proud circle till it fell into the orderly's hands. As it fell for the last time the last of the landing craft, its sides lined with silent British troops, moved slowly away from Palestine.

It was a quick and neat operation. At first light this morning there were nearly 3000 men on the shore. They withdrew as if they were quitting a battle. They took no chances. The Grenadiers and Coldstreamers came first along the empty streets. They marched in section formation straight on to the quay and on to their troopships. They carried their bayonets fixed and their rifles loaded. Cromwell tanks stood at the cross-roads with their engines ticking over and their guns moving to and fro, feeling for danger. As the troops passed their platoon billets on the slopes of Mount Carmel, the little faded Union Jacks were whipped down and the sentries left their posts and joined in. They left no flags behind. The port was surrounded with a rim of machine-gun posts manned by men of 40 Marine Commando in full battle kit. This unit fought in Dieppe, Sicily, and Anzio and was the last to leave the Holy Land.

By nine o'clock the town was empty of British soldiers and only the Commandos and the General remained in the port. The huge troopships Eastern Prince and Ocean Vigour put out to sea. Three L.C.T.s swallowed up the last of the tanks and trucks. They closed the big doors in their square bows and away they went abroad, singing and laughing like children released from a difficult term at school. No Jews went into the streets to wish them God-speed.

As the troops closed into the port 140 specially picked Jewish policemen took over the empty camps and harbour installations. They closed and locked gates that the British had guarded so long. They watched the final ceremony with expressionless faces. None saluted.

Formally the Jews took over the harbour. The British handed over a working port. There were no demolitions. One of the Jewish port administrators said: 'Everything is in excellent condition. There has been practically no damage at all.'

And an American officer supervising the withdrawal for the United Nations said 'Everything is in perfect condition – I am most impressed.' The camp furniture remained as the soldiers had left it. On the cookhouse wall yesterday's menu was still chalked up. A few orders still flapped on the notice-boards. A sign still pointed the way to St. Andrew's Church of Scotland. A dozen disconsolate dogs mooned around the quays, left behind by the soldiers. In all Haifa they alone showed any signs of regret.

The Observer, June 1948

Greece: notes on a civil war

"In 1948 I was covering the Greek guerrilla war and remember driving with Patrick to the front. He was a somewhat incongruous figure. He wore a loud toothcheck cap and mumbled as our jeep dodged mine craters and disembowelled mules. "Konitza lies on the lap...on the slope... in the arms... pinned against..." He was already writing his piece. To stop this mumbling I asked him, 'Patrick, where would you like to be at this moment if you could be transported there?' 'Entering the Brompton Oratory in my best Sunday clothes,' he replied without hesitation."

Mary Henderson, former correspondent for *Time and Life*.

Athens... There are very few people really starving in Athens. True, there are strange bony youngsters who carry little shaven death's heads on their shoulders in the shanty slums that creep like a disease across the plain of Attica. But for most there are black olives and black bread; and there is always the warm Attic sun. They manage.

The Minister of Foreign Affairs drives up to his Ministry in a car lent him by the French Embassy. He caresses his Civil Servants, tweaks their ears and prods their ribs as if they were old friends; 40 of them have not been paid for four months. Each month the chief of one of his departments gets enough to buy two pairs of shoes and a decent meal for one. The Prime Minister, eighty-eight years old, a twinkling, brave little old man, sits in a dingy office like the smoking room of a provincial club. He pays elaborate lip-service to the 'wisdom' of the American Mission. He says the American generals are right when they say the troubles will be over by the spring. Like every other Greek he knows perfectly well they are wrong.

Down in the markets under the cliff of the Acropolis, which wears its temples like a diadem, the antique shops are open. You can buy exquisite Turkish coffee pots, or gold and silver ikons where the Virgin in a huge Byzantine crown lifts her infant as if he were the Sacrament, or where strange, gaunt, eastern saints perform unheard-of wonders with angels and winged beasts. For these the accommodating Greek will ask perhaps two or three gold pounds. It means that he, like the Prime Minister and the Papadopulos family, distrusts the currency and fears for the future of his country. The pound is 20,000 drachmas. The gold pound is around 10 times that. Here in Greece they believe that the next war has already begun on Greek soil. They are already acting in the selfish, instinctive way that people do when faced with utter disaster. And of all people the Greeks are acquainted with disaster. They will act that way because they must until the fundamental split in Europe has been closed.

Superficially at least, Athens is as normal a city as any in Europe. The game of politics is still played as an end in itself. Cabinets are shuffled like football teams and appraised in the same spirit. Constitution Square is still cluttered with tables in a way no Anglo-Saxon municipality would tolerate. Oranges and tangerines are ripening on its trees. In the middle of the day the whole square is dark with Athenians sipping coffee or carefully watering their milk-white *ouzo*. Noise of talk as they call for newspapers or shout opinions into one another's faces all but drowns the noise of motor horns. And in the evening they walk to and fro across the square watching the sun go down behind the Acropolis in a sky that is as red as a cardinal's hat and twice as splendid. Towards the repellent new cathedral the Soho of Athens' narrow streets are sweet with the smell of tangerines and roasted chestnuts. The taverns are full, for a glass of *ouzo* is one of the few things that cost less than 1,000 drachmas. There is a little music there, too, perhaps from an old man with a guitar who, for a handful of crumpled notes, will sing you half a dozen songs of Crete or Epirus. And then the rest of the room will stop talking politics and smile and clap their hands and turn towards the old performer as he mumbles his songs under unshaded lights and across the spit-pocked floor.

There is no discernible sign that the Army is at war in the north. The elegant middle-aged men, thick-set, monocled, grey-homburged, and pin-striped, who wander over carpets of the Grande Bretagne Hotel will display a perfunctory curiosity in the activities of their Army in much the same way as other men display their gold watches. Their women – elegant and contemporary in the New Look – are even more bored with this remote brawl. There are few posters appealing for Service widows' and soldiers' comforts stuck on the walls of Government offices. There are a few Greek soldiers completely equipped from bootlaces to caps G.S. from British or American stores. There are a lot of foreign correspondents, and that is all.

But up in the north there is a vicious little frontier war in which a small town has been saved by real heroism. There is a bitter, ruined, countryside where the Athenian writ scarcely runs, where it is impossible to say whether the pathetic villages have been ruined by war or poverty, where men join the Communists because there is simply nothing else to do. The Greeks realise that this is for them an insoluble problem. They can contain the fighting more or less indefinitely. But in fact it is like the little running ulcer on a man's leg that is a sympton of a deep-seated disorder – in this case the relations of East and West. Until a greater physician than they are does something it must continue to run and run. Athenian reaction, which is understandable enough, is to enjoy their incomparable city and pretend they have no legs.

The Observer, 18 January 1948

From Greece he worked his way through the Far East, pausing in Malaya, where British forces were still fighting, reaching China, where the civil war was nearing its climax as he described in his book For Fear of Weeping.

Serving Mass in China, Christmas 1948

While I was sending my story, Bill [Sydney Smith] had found and called upon a Jesuit mission, and they had asked us to spend the feast of Christmas with them. We arrived in the dark. We had three rooms, all ice-cold, decorated with dark furniture, with *prie-dieu* and pictures of the saints. Somewhere in the house they were singing a carol. These Jesuits lived in an ugly collection of dark buildings on the far side of the city and the high Gothic walls that rose out of the slum were pierced with narrow windows. The Fathers, who were all Italian, received the three of us at supper. We dined in the refectory, a large cold room full of shadows. In black Chinese gowns, the Italian fathers sat in a hollow square eating the thin meal which was the end of their Advent fast. The Bishop of Pengpu sat between us at the top table under an enormous cross. He knew I was a Catholic and when some extra fried eggs were set in front of us he leaned forward and in Latin dispensed me from the discipline. A Chinese priest was reading in Latin from the Acts of the Apostles and in utter silence the old men, most of whom had not seen home for twenty years, sat munching their bread, their huge white beards rising and falling all around the edge of the room. There was an atmosphere of heroic simplicity. The bare cleanliness, the order and quiet and kindliness made an overwhelming contrast to the careless suffering we had watched for the last two days.

That night the cathedral was hung with cheap red silk, which in China is the fortunate and happy colour. It was a very ordinary and drab church, like a chapel in any Midland slum. Chinese texts had been hung from the pillars and the altar was covered with green branches. At ten o'clock that night they baptised twelve adult Chinese into the Church. The Bishop asked me if I would like to be their god-father, and so when my colleagues had gone to sleep, I stood in the freezing cathedral standing sponsor to these twelve young men. I remember that, feeling cold and tired and perhaps a little resentful, I gave them the old Celtic names. Somewhere in Communist China, if they still call themselves Christians, there are twelve men who bear such names as Brendan, Kilian, Rumold and Declan. One by one they were led by the foreign priests up to that poor altar. The priests wore scarves and overcoats under their copes as they breathed upon them and blessed and sprinkled and made them Christians.

I do not think I was ever more prepared for sleeping when the Bishop knocked at the door. He said they were just starting their midnight Mass. 'I would take it as a favour if you were to come and show them that the Church is really universal. It is a long time since they have seen any European who is not a priest take the Sacrament. I would be grateful if you would serve my Mass and go to Communion in front of them all. Father John, next door, is ready to hear your confession.'

Father John was a Maltese priest, a humble, snuffy old man who pulled his forelock whenever he saw the Bishop, whose British citizenship was his greatest source of pride, who hated Mussolini as if he had been a demon sent to catch the faithful. So once again I entered the cathedral and knelt down. It was not quite full. There was curfew outside and occasional shooting in the streets. At the back of the church there was a heap of bedding, and above the smell of incense and of wax there was a smell of poverty and unwashed wool which was probably as pleasing to God. The Chinese knelt in complete absorption.

Early next morning an officer from General Liu Shih's headquarters called on us at the Jesuit Mission. He presented the General's compliments and said that if we wanted to be sure of getting back to Nanking we should use a special train leaving that day. The Jesuits were singing the Mass for Christmas morning before the tawdry altar. The cathedral was packed almost beyond endurance. Standing, kneeling, clustered in the galleries, hundreds of Chinese stared towards the altar. Ugly old men at the back were leading them in prayer and the Mission resounded with the strange buzzing chant they had adapted from the Buddhists.

The Observer, December 1948

By May 1948 Nanking had fallen. Patrick wrote in The Observer: 'Without a motion of defiance, or tragedy, Nanking has been abandoned like an old tent. The Communists are pouring across the River Yangtze at six places on a 150-mile front.'
The British destroyer Amethyst was trapped on the Yangtze, and

on 23 April Patrick had cabled: 'Unless the Communist commanders on the river bank relent, there is only a small chance of recovering HMS Amethyst. This ugly fact is the climax of three days of unexpected violence on the Yangtze… No final explanation has ever been attempted here of what has happened. The British authorities have little to say, and information is sadly confused. Yet increasingly it is believed that the assault was not a decision of the local commander – such aberrations do not last three days. Rather it is a cold decision made by the People's Government in North China – which has already repudiated the Republic's treaties with the United States – that it would put a stop to the use of Chinese inland waters by foreign vessels of war.'

By the end of 1949 Shanghai was in Communist hands and Patrick, in Hong Kong en route for home, wrote of two small but significant incidents in particular and the situation in general.

A tale of two Englishwomen

Hong Kong… Many wise men believe the revolution in China is no more than a ripple on that deep pool of history. These old traders in their thin white suits bent over their gin and water in the dark bars of distant clubs will tell you it is a big ripple but it will pass, and, as always, leave China as it was before. This belief is comforting but almost certainly untrue. For Communism is as new to them as it is to the mass of China. It is changing China fundamentally, whether for the better it is still too early to say. But it is inviting disaster to pretend that we still have to face nothing stronger than a new version of the old.

I have seen two incidents in this war, incidents so small, so local, and so unimportant that neither history nor the local papers will record them. But they point to the difference that the merchants missed. A little while ago, when Shanghai was unwillingly prepared for its ordeal, an Englishwoman on the edge of the city had a garden and a half-timbered house with an iron lantern over the door. It might well have stood on the edge of any golf course in England but for the ancient garden with its old twisted trees, little painted Chinese bridge and long swelling lawns. But the house lay half a mile outside the defences. Just down the road, there was a mud pill box and a gate in the tall wooden wall Nationalists had built around the city to exclude the Communists.

One day four Nationalist soldiers strolled into the house telling the Englishwoman they had come to cut down the trees to improve their defensive position. She protested and they went. Later a captain came and, after accepting a reasonable present, he also left. The next day a colonel came and said they would at least have to remove the bamboo fence, but nothing happened for a week. Then one night a general telephoned – the Englishwoman was of some influence – and said that of course no one would touch the house or garden.

The next morning the garden was filled with several hundred soldiers not only hacking down the tall trees and the little flowering ones, but scything and carefully stamping in the flowers and jumping in dozens on the little bridge until it broke, laughing like naughty children in a play pit. Others were in the house trying the breakfast. One of the house servants was bleeding about the head and all the household were too frightened to move. Two soldiers were throwing clods at the windows in a reflective way while a captain had an armchair taken to the lawn with a tin of biscuits he had found.

The Englishwoman was told she must leave at once, taking no more than a suitcase. Later she took a lorry load of goods into the city and no one stopped her for long. By threats and bribery she almost cleared the house and took the stuff into Shanghai. The captain and his men moved into the house to help defend Shanghai and the cut trees lay where they had fallen, providing even more admirable cover for an enemy. It was all perfectly traditional.

In Tientsin, a similar thing happened when the Communists arrived. But it was a new pattern for China. The Englishwoman here had a house with an orchard and a company of infantry were billeted on her. There was no refusing. They marched in and the captain took an inventory of the house. Four days later they prepared to leave and the captain and the woman together checked the house. 'Is anything missing?' he asked. 'Nothing', she said, 'and I know of no other troops who could have behaved so correctly. Really, the only thing I can't find is a small face towel from upstairs. I am most grateful.' The captain interrupted her, paraded his men and searched their kits. One lad of nineteen had the towel, and he explained that he had packed it in error for his own. His comrades took him down to the orchard and shot him.

Apologising formally, the captain, as he left, gave the woman money for a new towel and for the burial of the young corpse at the bottom of her garden. They padded away and left the woman with a fistful of silver, and cold with horror at what had happened.

The Observer, May 1949

China: the nature of the change

Hong Kong... 'Get one of those fellows in the back of a Packard, stick a four-inch cigar in his mouth, and give him a bank account in hard currency and you'll find he's just the same as all the others. Goodness, man, they're Chinese even if they call themselves Communists.' If only one could be certain. If only one could know whether that heavy business man in the club bar, who distrusted journalists, was right or wrong. It is still the biggest question coming out of the Far East to confront the Western World. What is this new hard-faced China going to be like? In an hour or two a plane will take me away. This huge land mass and its vast population, which from its four thousand years of written history seems to have learnt little but how to suffer and endure what other nations have conquered, will sink away. All the evidence has been offered; it is time for a tentative verdict. We, whose business it was to watch this thing slowly creeping down from the north till it has almost engulfed the whole of China, are almost unanimous. What has happened here, the coming of Communism to this hopeless people, is one of the great climacterics of human history, which will change its course as surely and perhaps as deeply as the coming of Christ changed Europe, and the conquests of Muhammad the Middle East.

Already a fundamental change seems to have been produced in the young men who compose the Communist armies.

These new little men who pattered without military bands into Nanking and Shanghai did not loot, threaten, rob, and casually spoil, as other Chinese armies have done. They accepted no gifts and insisted on buying even the hot water they took to comfort their stomachs, in the place of tea, from the hot-water shops, which are themselves a symbol of China's poverty. Any infringements of their terrible laws have met with swift deaths. It is ruthless and beastly, but quite new. And perhaps it is not entirely alien to the Chinese character. Centuries ago, under ruthless emperors, they had the most successful and autocratic political organisation in the world. Each man had his place, and reward and punishment were allotted for fulfilling it or leaving it unfulfilled.

The popular hero for this profoundly godless people is usually a gross and sensual creature to Western eyes, but above all strong and cunning. The man they admire and obey is a great ruler with a huge belly and deep drunken laugh, with dozens of concubines, hundreds of children, armies of retainers, who rewards his friends immoderately and punishes his enemies most terribly. Ruthless Communism and the local party leader are as likely as anything to fill this need in the Chinese character. It has already done far more than Chiang Kai-Shek's drab and phoney revolution. Perhaps we who were paid to stay and watch it saw it too close and too late. But surely that Kuomintang Government must be among the most corrupt the world has known. There were the huge disgraceful fortunes made by men like T. V. Soong – the bureaucratic capitalist – who, while in office, created monopolies in their own interest. Or soldiers like Ho Ying-Chin, the present Prime Minister in Canton, who all his life has held such posts as head of the Whampoa Military Academy, Adjutant-General to the Forces, Minister of War, and emerges a fabulous millionaire. Or wealthy Sun Fo, the ex-Premier, whose name trails a shroud. It is not only big men. There was no possibility of getting anything new or constructive done in Shanghai, so that patients had to bribe their way into hospitals and relatives had to use bribes to get their dead into cemeteries, and every city ordinance became a source of profit for someone and almost every magistrate was for sale; and the young university graduate lived in an atmosphere of dull frustration till he either went under or did the same, or fled to the

North and the Communists.

The Communists have set about changing this even as they continued their southward march. If they can clean China and remain clean themselves – as they show every sign of doing – then we have witnessed the rebirth of a nation.

But somehow we watched it almost without emotion. Both sides were so alien to us in their ideas and morality. It is so far away and the suffering and poverty could be blamed on no one but the Chinese themselves. Yet, though much of it was hateful, I shall not quickly forget China. I shall remember the rich crowded landscapes of South China, where tiny villages almost jostle one another in rice-fields, where decayed pagodas rise like tiny prayers out of a bunch of trees. I shall remember the slums behind the towering Bund in Shanghai, and the beggars whining like beasts, and the boy who died of cold one night outside my hotel. I shall remember the 30 babies in a dusty ward in Canton, all due for death before nightfall from tetanus. I shall remember the long dinner parties, where we drank hot wine from little porcelain bowls. I shall remember those endless lines of soldiers padding always away from battle. I shall remember the almost deserted Buddhas in the temples of Hangchow.

The Observer, May 1949

Back at home in his basement flat in Harley Street, Patrick described what it was like to be a foreign correspondent.

Representing Britain: the official and the journalist

Foreign correspondents are part of the furniture of a capital, as inevitable as a luxury hotel. You find them meeting and explaining the situation to one another at little tables in Europe or on the grass at the edge of confused Asiatic battlefields. You can almost tell how grave any crisis has become by the number that collect. They may sound interesting or boring to you, these rootless men just past their youth, talking of their trade in the bar they have chosen as theirs. Whichever they may be in real life, they have an alarmingly important role to play in a Parliamentary democracy. For correspondents of newspapers and broadcasting are the sole avenue of information open to all but Ministers and higher officials on what is happening outside this country. Even a member of Parliament has few other sources. The correspondent therefore has a considerable responsibility to society for the finding of facts and the explaining of remote situations – for pursuing truth – but he works under conditions that frequently make this almost impossible. He must work as an isolated individual among strangers, with all his resources in his suitcase and his head. He can rarely call on the organisation or authority of his newspaper for help in understanding a situation. Yet what he writes on a dressing-table in his hotel bedroom is given the weight of a national paper's name. And too often the reader cannot judge its truth or value by any known standard or personal experience.

Ideally, of course, a correspondent knows the details of a crisis before he approaches it. In fact this is seldom possible, particularly on an extended tour, say, in the East. And increasingly as the old organisation of society disintegrates, it is more difficult to collect truth. In at least two countries I have visited in the past six months, it was not possible to see any Minister of State or person in authority belonging to that country. In Rangoon, at that time, one British journalist was awaiting trial and possible death, and the others were regarded as little more than hostile agents. In Nanking, Ministers were preoccupied with obtaining accommodation in Formosa or with their own personal ruin. Their departments were deserted. (Their statements anyway were of little more than curiosity value, and bore no relation to the situation.) In these places, apart from watching the people walking the streets of their cities, the Press was dependent almost wholly upon the diplomatic corps for any sort of explanation of what was going on. In other places it was the same, but for a different reason: society had split into revolutionary and counter-revolutionary groups, and news had become merely another weapon.

In the East to-day, a correspondent stepping out of a 'plane into a strange situation turns first to the Embassy or Consulate. He visits the Press Officer (First Secretary probably), who inhabits a large department littered with familiar weeklies and full of foreign gentlemen typing hand-outs projecting the British Way of Life. The journalist – it is like the opening move in an old dance – will first be told that it is not the function of Press Officers to care for visiting pressmen, though in fact they are invariably anxious to help. Unfortunately it is in the nature of their job that their relations are chiefly with London, and of all the staff they probably know least about the local situation. When he comes to deal with the rest of the staff, the correspondent is met, only too often, by a deep suspicion that comes close to contempt.

This is not, of course, universally true; heads of missions are usually, but not always, frank and helpful. Where this is the case, the countries concerned get more intelligently reported in the English papers as a result. But the fact remains that to-day a British journalist in the East usually bases his political interpretation on the American representatives, who are more open-hearted, or perhaps on the Indians, who are usually able to offer a coherent, even if sometimes rather exotic, interpretation. This chilly attitude is particularly unfortunate for British colonies. For here the London newspapers have a special function: they are indeed one of the few checks on the local officials. The legislative Assemblies – I write of the East still – are unrepresentative. And the local Press is often too wild to count. Yet nowhere that I have been are officials more suspicious of the Press than in the territories we control in the East. Criticism has come to be regarded as close to disloyalty.

It seems high time that our official representatives, both diplomatic and colonial, had it explained to them that they are not more important than the public itself, whose unworthy but actual liaison it is our privilege to be.

The Observer, Autumn 1949

Patrick began a series of broadcasts about his favourite places in England, none more familiar or loved than his village, Marylebone.

Marylebone village

You had best get to Marylebone village by taking a tube train and getting out at Regent's Park. You will then arrive at the quietest and saddest station in London. It is an underground place of odd passages that end in sudden shadow and of large locked doors. It has a long winding staircase on whose walls people who do not come from Marylebone delight to be rude. And it has no less than three lifts which the porters use in turn, one at a time. You may be the only passenger. When you have crossed the ticket lobby upstairs, which is like the vestry of a rather unsuccessful church, dusty and dark and full of things, so that one expects a pile of hassocks, photographs of dead vicars and an inexpensive processional cross instead of the ticket machine – when you have crossed this lobby, walked up a tunnel and pushed against a blast of air that blows night and day into those empty galleries, you will have reached Marylebone. You have then only to avoid two old gentlemen selling evening papers in a rather hopeless way and a smart young man straight in front of you with a barrow of well-polished fruit and you will be there.

A great deal of London is still really a series of villages. There are long stretches where people just live because they have to and then suddenly you come upon a recognisable village or even a market town. There is one in Kensington and Chelsea and Stepney and Shepherd Market and there is at least one in Marylebone. Not so very long ago it really was a village surrounded by farms and country houses, and it still is in heart and fact a village with all the attributes of a village, though you might not notice it if you hurried past in a bus or a taxi. You would miss the little chatty crocodiles of girls from Queen's School in Harley Street, and the smiling nuns in clouds of black cloth from Cavendish Square, and Sydney Fitzjohn the milkman who has been here twenty years or more and knows it better than I do. I'd say he was the best known of anyone hereabouts; smiling, weather-beaten, busy.

It is a very clearly defined village and quite small. There is a crowded high street down the middle and on one side the quarter where the doctors live, which is the special trade of the place. There is Harley Street and Wimpole Street and

Weymouth Street and Devonshire Street and there are small impersonal back streets full of ritzy little nursing homes and small upper-class hospitals. This goes on as far as Great Portland Street where they sell the motor cars. On the other side of the High Street, it is rather less coherent. You get ambassadors and a superb museum in Manchester Square, but also there is a rather pleasant tangle of small streets and squares full of chapels with closed doors and hostels and discreet public houses and little fruit shops and newsagents whose windows contain dummy cigarette cartons – until you get to Baker Street. And the top and the bottom of the High Street end in two great crowded roaring roads, in Oxford Street at its most busy and in the Marylebone Road, full of cars preoccupied with getting out of London; and the two of them, like two rivers, effectively cut us off from the rest of London. I believe there are other villages on the other sides of these roads; there is a charming one beyond Baker Street which I have visited, but that is a very secret and inward looking one and no place for strangers.

The medical side of the High Street always seems to me to be among the most forbidding in London. Thousands of people must have been told behind those heavy painted doors that the limits of their lives were in sight, and these dark rectangular valleys, full of quiet traffic and of serious, busy people going somewhere else, have caught something of this atmosphere, the suggestion that life is a serious, dignified thing and that death is an incident to be met, not with extravagant horror or too much pity, but in a quiet clean room with decency.

I believe that originally these good farm lands were bought as a speculation by the Adam brothers at the end of the eighteenth century, and they laid it out in a bold plain plan of streets that all cross each other at right angles. The brothers, and others after them, built these tall houses, all a little alike, for the professional classes. Gladstone and Dickens lived hereabouts once and the Mr. Barrett who had the large family in Wimpole Street. This part of the village is nothing like so splendid as that great circle of houses round Regent's Park, that ring of white palaces that stare haughtily across the tall green trees, across the morose park-keepers and the children mucking up the flower beds and the fountains. But those are dead palaces now where the Ministry of Food does its secret work.

No, this quarter of our village is just good, plain, rather boring building; and, if you walk slowly, you see into the front ground-floor rooms, which is always interesting.

Not many of these houses are still used by single families. Hundreds of them have been cut up into flats, not luxury flats but flats for people who work hard and have done well and will probably work–if only because they cannot save–until they die. In their way, I would say these professional men probably make a greater single contribution to the good of society than any other group of individuals living together anywhere in England. But you cannot really generalise about them, because they are not a coherent class, but a collection of rather prickly individuals who do not know their neighbours. Some are killing themselves to send their sons to the schools their fathers chose for them; there are others whose youth was dominated by the necessity of passing countless examinations and have never relaxed or learnt to relax from this dreadful compulsion to fill every possible hour with more work; and there are others who came the easy way and must still struggle to survive, and there are a few, I fear, who live here and batten on the reputation of their neighbours. You don't often see all these people. But you can meet their wives in the High Street. You will see them with baskets on their arms, in plain sensible clothes, with maybe a short fur coat and a scarf against the cold winds that sweep down these straight streets carrying just a little freshness from the open park.

Further up the street, past a few public houses and the undertakers and some antique shops full of the most lovely glass in London, past an old-fashioned book-shop, a Belgian cake-shop crammed with lady villagers drinking coffee up to their ankles in piled parcels, you come to the fruit and vegetable shops. There is every sort of these. There is a traditional open-fronted shop with potatoes all over the floor and sprouts water-falling out of a tray and a delicious smell of mud and the country, or there is another with a lot of plate glass and an antiseptic atmosphere with assistants in white. There is a fishmonger with the most talkative salesman in London, some more pubs and a corner grocer with its windows solidly wall-ed with biscuit tins, and finally, just as there should be, there is the village draper's and a general store. This is one of my favourite places. The windows are piled high with little mountains of sensible things. And it is a sensible place that depends more on its old connection with the village than on any modern salesmanship or slick display. It is pleasantly full inside with housewives who know their business – though there may be a rather tiresome titled lady ordering three lawn handkerchiefs to be sent to an address in Suffolk. There will be middle-aged women sitting opposite an assistant while he measures yards of curtain material on a polished strip of brass let into the counter. And there is an overwhelming smell of clean linen and a low hum of talk, and in the linen, lace and ribbon department there is still a high Victorian machine for getting your change. The assistant takes your money, wraps it in the bill, pops the little bundle into a wooden ball and places the ball in a tiny lift. He pulls a string and, ping, up it shoots towards the ceiling and the ball rumbles off down a small mahogany railway over the shoppers and piles of eiderdowns and saucepans and pram covers, rumble, rumble, until it reaches a desk, a high commanding desk where a sort of queen of the retail trade sits with her neat head against the ceiling. She unscrews the ball, pops back the change and back comes the ball, rumble, rumble, over the pram covers, the saucepans and the eiderdowns, and lands with a small crash in its little cage, and the purchase is complete. There will probably be a farthing among the change. There always is when I go.

Then there is the 'local' in a mews that still smells a little of horses. It has a friendly brown front and a lamp in an old frame that was put there for a fish-tailed gas jet. And inside it is full of the glitter of polished glass and flowers. It is used only by people who work or live round here, doctors and taximen and policemen and people from the B.B.C. It is a place for Sunday morning or half an hour of an evening. It has that special atmosphere shared by all good pubs, reassuring and simple and familiar and good. It is a place where you say, 'thank you' as you leave. On the other side of the High Street there is another special place. It is one of those old, half-forgotten London burial grounds. Councillors that died years ago have moved away the worn tombstones and set them like old soldiers on an annual parade all round the edge, hundreds of silvery grey slabs from which the names have long since disappeared. There are a few blackened flower-beds and a green thing like a small bandstand that no one uses. Typists eat their lunch there in the pale sunshine and children run shouting down its regimented asphalt paths. Old people from what used to be the workhouse sit quite alone looking at almost nothing, wrapped in their memories as if they were a shroud. And the high backs of buildings are turned to it on every side. It is charming and also rather terrible, this mixture of the generations. It is also an integral part of the village. They use it as the village green. *The Listener, 2 February 1950*

The next assignment was a year's tour of Africa, now just beginning to impinge on British consciousness after the war years when all thoughts were turned to Europe and the Far and Middle East.

South Africa: racial rumblings

*Johannesburg...*It is as if a ragged and despairing army had laid siege to the city. In the centre, Johannesburg sits on its gold reef as massive as a mountain. On three sides there are suburbs, scarcely more permanent than army camps. They creep over the low hills, squalid and lawless. Not that the citizens within are worried. They seem hardly aware of the camps outside their walls. In fact they think they are winning the siege; the White army is on their side, and already they have outflanked some of the Black camps, have built suburbs beyond and around them, and by the terms of the Group Areas Act – a big and undiscriminating gun – will one day force them to move on.

Of these sad dwelling places you may have heard of Sophiatown. One's first impression is of countless narrow doors opening on dark rooms; of ant-hill overcrowding, of noisy decay. It lies off the main road where the trams run. It is laid out as simply as a Roman camp; streets cross at right angles. The houses are little tattered bungalows. It is a place of fluttering rags. Women shout like sergeants down its streets, young men over-dress and go rotten. Too many people stand in the shade and do nothing. Most houses consist of a single room dominated by a bed, with perhaps a few pious pictures on the wall and a photograph of Royalty. Paper and stone lie on the roads because they are seldom cleaned. Its citizens come from all over the lower half of Africa. Down its centre runs Victoria Road. It is as ragged as the rest. Indian shops have wire mesh across their windows. There are many chapels, mere front rooms where African preachers have invested in some eccentric aspect of Christ, have nailed a board on their wall and painted a cross on their door and twice a week preach to women a mixture of Christianity and Black nationalism.

Some 80,000 people live here, sleeping more than one family to a room and sub-letting against the law. There are no drinking shops, but women brew beer in basins under their beds. It is not safe at night. Smart young men without jobs and in cheap American suits, with wide-brimmed hats turned up all the way round, stand on corners to assault strangers or rob workers of their pay packets. Priests in this town are not called to the dying at night. They wait until morning. Among these houses there are even meaner houses. I went to one built of squashed oil drums. Its tenant leant against his door filing a piece of his bicycle. He came from Basutoland. He earned £8 a month in a dairy – fine wages for an African. Each month he paid £1. 5s for the hutch in which he could not stand upright. He would not look up nor smile, nor in any way declare his heart. His woman was cooking in a bucket on wood, and his children were scratching naked at a game in the hard earth.

These towns certainly are a by-product of Africa's change. Yet something might be done for these people if it were recognised that they represent a major part of the nation's greatest problem. But the Government is pre-occupied with other things: like a man resting in a cloud of flies and anxious to dream, it flaps at them to drive them off.

The Africans must carry passes to prove that they are in work or have the right to work, or else they must return to the villages they left in despair. They are subject to a curfew as if they had recently been conquered. They are, of course, without votes and they cannot bear arms in any army.

In Sophiatown I went into one hut. A woman from Bechuanaland dressed in a blanket and suckling a child opened the door. For a few feet up, the walls were of mud – the rest was of rusted tin. There were holes in the roof. She had a narrow bed and a pile of blankets for three other children that slept on the floor. There was a pile of tins in the corner in which she cooked. Her husband works for the municipality; it takes him an hour and a half to get to and from his work. Such huts, adequate for chickens, filled the valley; around them the bush veld stretched away as limitless and uneventful as the sea; and above, the blue emptiness of the South African sky.

This army of rootless men has no part in the wealth or pride of South Africa. If such an army were camped outside my city I should fear for the future of my people.

The Observer, 17 September 1950

Sinister castles in Africa

Gold Coast… There is a row of castles down the edge of Africa. They never defended much more than the dividends of a foreign trade. Yet on the Gold Coast [now Ghana], on some 200 miles of sea shore, there are more than forty of them, Portuguese, Dutch, British, German, Swedish, and Danish. These are the old traders' castles. Some of them are 500 years old, some less than a hundred. Many are ruined, most are empty, and oddly, little is known of their sinister history. For some 400 years the foreign traders with a handful of fever-rotten soldiers were virtually prisoners in these places. The Europeans never left the coast to go inland, but waited for the African kings to send gold and ivory and skins for which they gave trade goods. They also waited here for the main commodity of the coast trade, the tens of thousands of slaves to be packed in the holds of ships and sent across the sea to the Americas and the West Indies.

Today the British Governor of the Gold Coast lives in one of these castles on the outskirts of Accra. It is tall and graceful like a tropical version of Hamlet's Elsinore, with sheer walls which rise straight out of the long Atlantic breakers. It is called Christiansborg and the Danish crown is still cut above the great door. When his Excellency entertains he does so over the dark and vaulted cellars, still with their iron doors and barred windows, where men and women waited for months for a ship to take them away for ever.

In the eighteenth century a local chief obtained possession of

Christiansborg. He wore the uniform of the Danish governor, and when he entertained had 21 guns to fire him salutes from the battlements. He sold it to the British. They used it for a little as a lunatic asylum and then restored it and made it their Government House.

But most of the castles stand empty today, ruined by the closing of the slave trade. There is usually a little mud fishing village close by and a row of painted canoes drawn up under their walls. Here the traders lived an appalling life. They died early of fever, drink, and violence. They fought and betrayed one another. The wars between them were fought here without any sort of chivalry. The Portuguese took the British for galley slaves; the British mutilated a Dutch garrison. The diminutive garrisons were mostly convicts sent out to die, swelter in red coats, and forced to buy their provisions from their master. Wars were conducted by setting one tribe against another, which at least stimulated the production of slaves.

The most splendid of these castles is Elmina which stands like a stone crown on a point of land, rising out of leaning palms and edged with surf. The Portuguese brought out the tower stone by stone in the holds of their ships from Lisbon 500 years ago. It has been fought for many times. There is a great yard surrounded by dark galleries for the male slaves and another, very deep and narrow, for the females. There is a bridge which crosses a creek leading to the tall walls and as the slaves crossed it they would throw their little gold ornaments into the water, praying the river god to ensure their safe return. He was a faithless god. In all the world there can be few buildings that have seen more misery and useless death than these empty walls in Africa.

The Observer, March 1951

Christmas beside a hot lagoon

Lagos... Across the door, in a barely perceptible wind, the bead curtains are clicking like false teeth; the fan in the ceiling has been turning all day. In the street, dark-faced men in white gowns are strolling very slowly past the stalls that sell combs and scent and mangoes. There is little noise of traffic, only that ancient noise a city makes in the sun, the murmur in unison of thousands of voices, the sudden sound of a man shouting in anger behind a wall, dogs barking and cocks crowing, the steady thud thud from women grinding millet in a wooden bowl.

This city is neither old nor beautiful. Time has not treated it gently, but seems to have torn at it with nails as it passed by. The pavements are broken, the shutters hang crooked, electric wires make a careless web across the front of buildings, the mean houses peer over each other's shoulders without plan or grace. Beyond the city there is a wide lagoon crossed by an iron bridge, and little boats, like willow leaves on the water, are waiting there for fish. Beyond the lagoon there is a vast, unfamiliar sea, and beyond the sea – how many miles to the edge of Europe – is England.

That gigantic Dispersal which has scattered men and women from the United Kingdom along many shores of the world has left a fair-sized community here. Like others who have exiled themselves for as many motives as there are men, they are apt to suffer from a small and rooted sorrow. It is an unease that somehow seems to lend an extra dignity and meaning to their lives. I do not think that, even if they could, they would pluck it out. Most of them are a little sick for home. Some will not return because of what they fear to find there; some profess to dislike the place because of the Government, or the decadence of the working class, or because it rains; most can return only rarely since they lack the means. Yet towards the end of every year there comes this gentle sorrow.

Christmas at home is not a sentimental cliché here. For somehow, under all the vulgarity and ugliness with which we have covered it, it remains the family feast, the celebration of one's first loyalties and loves. It is a time when one takes one's pleasures simply and in private, and the people who dislike Christmas are those who have lost such tastes or to whom they are for ever denied by some chance or tragedy.

I do not often spend Christmas at home. One year it was in a mission house in China with the doors locked and the windows barred because the town outside was being looted and the Communists were expected before the New Year; another was in Bethlehem when Arabs shot at the car out of the darkness and the congregation was all soldiers; and another was in a cold railway carriage between Düsseldorf and Hamburg at a time when the dust-grey ruins of Germany still presented the worst that man could do to man. But it was always different from any other time.

Soldiers in danger seem usually to treasure some special corner of their country and to remember it continually as a sort of reassurance against the unnatural nonsense that surrounds them. I remember one who loved the front of Blackpool as passionately as ever Ulysses loved Ithaca, although he never saw it for more than five days in the year and that only in a year when no child was born to him; and there was another who came very close to poetry when he spoke of riding in a Salford tram of a Saturday night. The business of Christmas is much the same. For every man it is a private vision or nothing at all. This feast that takes place behind locked doors has little to do with the phoney symbolism of trees and tinsel displayed each year about a month in advance by the larger shops.

Now mine is a London Christmas with the streets so empty that, from the far end, you can hear a man walking home from church and you see slopes in the road that you never remembered. There are the snatches of carols, execrably sung by commercially-minded children, that still suggest a little of the solemnity and difference of the tail-end of the year. There is the walk across the threadbare park after luncheon (no – it is dinner at Christmas) with dozens of others doing the same, each clearly pre-occupied with the same private discomfort, each walking alone in preparation for the unwanted cake at tea. There are the Christmas cards, often hideous in themselves, which represent the evidence of some friend or acquaintance.

But somehow, Christmas at home is more than the sum of all these details. Among the Churches it is by no means the greatest feast of the year, but it still represents the gentlest and most lovely idea that mankind ever conceived, more beautiful than Aphrodite and her waves, or Buddha and all his struggles for perfection. Even if you have discarded its Christian content, it still celebrates the perfect family. A man and his wife who at this time of the year can surround themselves with their own people in their own home within their own city or village, seem to me the most enviable in the world. More than the delicious pleasures of being rich or in the Cabinet, they have the most massive and natural pleasure of all.

We shall have our Christmas here beside the hot lagoon. Some of us will celebrate the birth of Christ, and almost all of us will think of some special corner of Britain. But however devout or gay we become, we shall not be at home.

The Observer, 24 December 1950

In April 1952 he went to Korea. He remained there till December 1953.

Korea: unforgettable fragments of the picture

Panmunjom... It is customary at the new year for broadcasters and journalists publicly to display a little optimism and a great deal of good will. Just for a little there settles a mood that is a pale reflection of the sweetest – and most prostituted – feast in all religion. But somehow this year it does not seem to settle so easily, particularly in the Far East. At the risk of distorting the picture of a situation that is already twisted enough, I have to say – writing this at Panmunjom before leaving for New Zealand – that almost all the things I shall remember of this year were terrible. True, the Coronation made a distant rumble of splendour; but it were better that the things that stuck in the memory here should never have happened.

The fragments of the picture are not easy to forget. There was that single file of United States Marines struggling upwards to take the crown of a minor hill. I watched them all one morning, staring safely through a concrete embrasure with a cup of coffee in my hand. They moved very slowly in a majestic uproar of explosions. They often lay pressed against the ground. The dirt leapt upwards and around them like great waves against a sea groyne. They went up and lay for a little close to the dreadful summit. They came down and tried once more and then withdrew, slowly, as if they were struggling through a storm. And the whole shape of the hill had been changed and the file was smaller when it got back.

And then, perhaps illogically, the Turkish soldier seemed to matter. He was a small anonymous man whose padded coat trailed on the ground. On the first day of the exchange of sick and wounded prisoners he threw himself out of an ambulance and into the arms of an American major, embraced him as if he had come to a brother he had despaired of ever seeing again, held him and wept. He refused to let go, though General Mark Clark was plucking at his elbow to welcome him. No one smiled and it was not embarrassing. Later there were three American soldiers, just back from prison, sitting in a row looking shaken and subdued, their hair still powdered with insecticide. They were talking to a crowd of journalists, and one of them asked the sergeant if he personally knew of anyone who had 'betrayed his buddies.' The sergeant said, 'Do you really want to know?' and the reporter said, 'Yes.' The sergeant said, 'There's one sitting right next to me,' and the wretched boy went white and scrambled off the bench and hurried through the silence out of the tent.

There were the children. It was at the beginning of this year. The place was Seoul, and the icy wind was like a continuing physical pain. The building had been a Japanese temple and was little more than a shell. It housed some of the hungry and frequently delinquent little orphans who ran wild through the broken city. The director led the way upstairs and pulled back a sliding screen to show a room that must have been as dark as any cupboard when the screen was closed. At first the place seemed empty. Then you saw that five small boys had 'swarmed' in a corner. They were standing clustered against one another facing the wall. They did not look round. They wore thin, trailing rags. They were unimaginably dirty and their hair was pale with dirt. They stood there shaking, pressed against a lukewarm radiator. Two of them were weeping without making any noise. When I brought out some chocolate, they fought to get the largest share.

It was the most terrible place for children I have ever seen. In the corridors, wherever a pipe ran from ceiling to floor, there would be a frightened, silent, incurious child just standing. In another room they sat in rows on the floor, huddled in blankets, and they refused to uncover their faces. The kitchen was a stone basement lit by candle light, and there was ice on the floor. In another room twelve boys were filling matchboxes by hand. The place stank of drains and boiled barley. Despite a guard of bigger, better-dressed boys, a high proportion of the boys ran away back to their ruins until the police rounded them up again. The director was unpaid and you could not blame him because he sometimes sold things that soldiers gave for the children. When I revisited this place, a few days ago, the director had gone and the place was run by a relief organisation. Windows were mended and rice replaced the barley. The guards at the gate had gone and the children no longer ran away. When we walked into the yard, someone blew a bugle out of a window and all the children came running out laughing, dressed approximately as Boy Scouts, to salute the flags of South Korea and America. They do it several times a day for visitors.

And then there was the hatred. Curiously, this was never so apparent during the fighting. You had to go to the wide valley behind the Chinese lines to see it naked. Here at Panmunjom for fourteen months, and almost ritually, was celebrated that new and very articulate hatred that a large part of the East now feels for the West. It was certainly disturbing. The Communist delegates would sweep past with set expressions. Their journalists would wait with us on the same road and, with the exception of the two English-speaking ones who had their mission to perform, they would speak to no one. Each man stood alone, took no notes, almost as if wrapped in some private sorrow. The conference concerned peace, but there was no trace of the behaviour that visitors to youth festivals report.

Nothing of supreme importance was decided at Panmunjom. The delegates merely registered and administered the calculated moves that had been made elsewhere. But if anyone still believes that things are not terribly changed in the Far East, a few visits to this village that no longer exists would be enough to convince him. Of course, one could certainly find something more appropriate to the season in the quiet beauty of Japan, in the activities of soldiers at Christmas time, or in the shining good intentions of the Indians who came to help. But these things happened in Korea, and Korea was the outward and visible sign of the world's deep sickness. And to write of anything else from this part of the world would seem a little insincere and silly.   *The Observer, 27 December 1953*

He was in England when Winston Churchill died.

Churchill's funeral

The procession took that most ancient road that runs from the Palace of Westminster to the steps of the Cathedral of St. Paul. It is a road that half the history of England seems to have taken, on its way to a crowning or to a public and ignoble death, to murder or be murdered, to raise revolt, to seek a fortune, or to be buried. The route was lined with young soldiers, their heads bowed over their automatic rifles in ceremonious grief. The great blocks of troops crunched past over the sanded road. The bands played old and slow tunes. The drums were draped in black. The staffs of the drum-majors were veiled. They moved slowly, steadily, at a curiously inexorable pace, and it looked as if nothing could ever stop them. They moved through a tangible silence and the great crowd, not quite as cold as death itself, watched with an eloquent and absolute silence.

It was beautiful in the way that great works of art are beautiful. It obeyed secret rules. It was dignified and cast a dignity about it. There were the familiar and expected surprises. There was the Earl Marshal walking alone and worried in the centre of a great space like any man lost in a high street, but carrying a gilded sceptre. There was Lord Mountbatten pacing behind the Chiefs of Staff carefully manipulating his sword and, like any trooper, trying to keep pace with the band. There were the officers with their trays of Churchill's medals, held out like ware for sale. There were the heraldic banners of the Cinque Ports and the Spencer-Churchills, too stiff to wave in any wind, carried like trophies before the coffin. And there were the marshals with their batons held on their hips in a baroque gesture that Marlborough would have known. There was the family looking lost and human and trying to keep up. There were the anonymous coaches filled with women. But the central, the overwhelming fact was the dead body in a box made of oak. There was no getting away from that. It was trundled into the City on a huge and impractical gun-carriage. It was pulled by a great phalanx of lusty young men. It moved, huge and red with the Union flag, past the hotels and the steamy restaurants and the newspaper offices and the pubs, surrounded by this extraordinary silence that could not be broken even by the bands and the rhythmic feet. It was a silence, not of grief but of respect. In fact the City was stopped and was turned into a theatre and it was all performed as a drama that all men understand. Commentators all over the world have reached for their explanations. This was the last time that such a thing could happen. This was the last time that London would be the capital of the world. This was an act of mourning for the Imperial past. This marked the final act in Britain's greatness. This was a great gesture of self-pity and after this the coldness of reality and the status of Scandinavia.

But really this was a celebration. And however painful, most funerals are just that. When a man is buried, those who are still alive crave some gesture of respect that cannot help the cadaver. And this gesture is made over and over again by Christians and Communists and humanists and the unconcerned. It is a proud half-conscious assertion that man is not an animal that dies alone in a hole. It is almost a gesture of contempt to the face of death. And once or twice in a generation a dead monarch or hero is chosen to epitomise a whole nation's assertion of continuity and dignity. And because Churchill at a certain time and in a special way was, for all public purposes, Britain and more than Britain, this assertion was unbelievably eloquent over his corpse.

This was a celebration, then, of our humanity and of the fact of Britain. But Britain just now is a curious country. It is the only country where patriotism is dismissed as a joke in bad taste and where treason, or what once passed for treason, is the fashionable manner of writing and talking. It is the one country where intellectually to destroy and to reject has taken the place of longing to build and create. And we give a lead in this respect which no other people in the world seems anxious or interested to follow. In this respect alone, in this strange and temporarily unhappy setting, the great funeral was eccentric. And yet it happened and despite all the watching television cameras, the crowds came out and stood in all the old awe. The ritual, performed to music like a masque for the edification of a king, said things that cannot quite be put into words. The whole country watched the agonised care of the eight guardsmen who carried the box. And vicariously shared their anxious pain. But perhaps most marvellous was the slow move up the turgid Thames. There were things like the gantries of cranes dipping in salute and the music of a host of pipers. There were generals in improbable uniforms and what looked like all the rulers of the world standing on the steps of St. Paul's as if this were a family burial. A whole city looking in on itself as a dead body went by.

It was a triumph. It was a celebration of a great thing that we did in the past. It was an act of gratitude to a man whom we can no longer help or please. The many Heads of State there were appropriate but not important. We were not sad. We knew for whom these bells tolled. We knew the man whose body we removed in such unimaginable splendour. And we did not weep – that is not fitting for great old men – but we saw him off and because he was us at our best, we gave him a requiem that rejected death and was almost a rejoicing.

The Observer, 31 January 1965

Washington: the city whose business is government

This article is about the City of Washington. It will be empty at the centre because it is not about 'the President'. At any single moment of the day there will be 10,000 people discussing him, telling a new story about him with the usual odd mixture of admiration and disapproval. But the fact remains that all around him and in his shadow there is a great city which will be there after he has gone – impossible thought – and which works to strengthen his hand – as if it needed it – and which still manages to maintain a semi-independent life of its own – but only just.

The purpose of this town is government, and in the process of governing and talking and writing about governing, an intricate social pattern has emerged. It is true that there is an hereditary aristocracy here, known as the 'cave dwellers', hidden away in Georgetown mansions, scanning the Senate without hope for men who are socially possible, but they have no influence. Theirs is a secret aristocracy recognised only among themselves. To be sure of social acceptance here you must be connected with the Congress, the Central Intelligence Agency, the White House, the Supreme Court, the Diplomatic Corps or have a liberal-minded column in a newspaper. It is hopeless if you are a civil servant who commutes to a split-level ranch-type house in a Maryland suburb. It is hopeless if you are a Negro (more than half those in the city are), a junior officer in the Forces, a clergyman (unless you are a Dean of the Episcopalian Cathedral), a professor in any one of Washington's five universities, work in an Embassy whose motherland cannot be instantly found on a map, or do anything that has no connection with politics. You may be rich and your dining-room chairs authentic Chippendale, and you may even have a Picasso and a Gainsborough, but it will not help. There are exceptions to these stern rules, but not many.

It is not that it is a snobbish town, but it is one regulated by function. Introductions tend to specify with admirable clarity the precise job of each stranger. The only exception to this is the Central Intelligence Agency, whose young men in well-cut suits and black thin ties tend to murmur that they are 'in government.' But everyone knows. The Congressional and the diplomatic set meet only at the top. On the whole, the hordes of eager, ambitious, mop-haired First, Second and Third Secretaries entertain colleagues, dutifully reporting their hospitality to justify their allowances. The other horde of eager ambitious, crew-cut young men who work for Senators and Congressmen and who plan one day to supplant them, make a different, equally professional world in which their intelligence is masked by their devotion to the job in hand.

Unlike London, where the embassies seem to get lost in the swirls of the city, they stand out here as pinnacles of social grandeur. The Embassies of France, Britain, Italy and Spain tower over the others. I would not dare to try to grade them. At vast expense, the Ambassadors offer up their livers almost every night in the service of their country. There can be surely nowhere else in the world so addicted to giving parties. No one even pretends to like them. They are a way of life, sanctified by usage rather than usefulness. It is true that he has set his countenance against them, but they survive.

Now there are special techniques proper to a Washington

cocktail party. The ceremonial giants, Ambassadors, Senators, Justices of the Supreme Court, are austerely moderate, come late and leave early. They never – well, hardly ever – misbehave. For these parties are not fun, they are business. Or, more accurately, you dare not miss them if you are on the make yourself. When you walk into a drawingroom crowded with hot people holding cold drinks, you greet first your hostess and then the servants. These will be distinguished Negroes whom you have met again and again at precisely similar functions. They belong to a gentle black Mafia of hired help. They whip up the canapés which they bring to the party on the back seats of their splendid cars. They carry buckets of ice as a doctor carries a black bag. They can tell at a glance if the drink supply is adequate. They are wildly expensive and are treated with profound respect. They do not gossip, though they have served at a thousand different tables. They are a corps of professionals without whom Washington could not survive. You know that you have begun to arrive when they begin to remember what you like to drink. There are also the vast shindigs given in hotels which may be for some obscure national day or the arrival of a celebrity with an expense account. Or every night there are countless dinner parties, hot, candle-lit, the product of a day's work on the part of the hostess and carefully designed to need the minimum of service, but, under the self-help, bearing a formality as strict as that of Versailles. Or there are buffet-suppers where the main course will be hot ham and a sweet sauce for certain, with a glass of *vin rosé* thrown in on the side. There are very few tea parties – everyone's too tired.

Of course this is not the whole of Washington. This is only the part that shows above the ocean of newsprint. There is that suburban Washington, eager in good works, philoprogenitive within reason, lawn-proud church members who take their wives out once a week for a steak dinner preceded by two jumbo martinis. At Christmas, the most extravagantly extrovert among them put a lifesize cut-out of Santa Claus and his reindeers on the roof. And floodlight it. Or there are the Negroes, silent in their hot slums. Perhaps 'silent', except politically, is not the word. You can tell when you leave the white areas. The street is more untidy. There are more people standing and talking. The liquor stores are seedier and there are more tin signs advertising popular soft drinks. The children stay up later. The front doors are open on dark hallways and the street windows open on rooms as full of beds as a Victorian hospital. You are not made to feel welcome. These people are janitors, servants, Government drivers, secretaries, transport workers, painters, or they move the packing cases around in warehouses. I do not think they will stay silent much longer.

Or there is the tourist's Washington – exhausting but exciting. Americans, like Muslims to Mecca, like to see Washington once before they die. Each summer an immense migration of schoolchildren takes place. They sleep packed like codlings in second-class hotels. They tramp round the Capitol, peer at the declaration of Independence, occasionally pop into the National Gallery, which is one of the greatest in the world and still getting better, patter in awe through the White House, visit the great necropolis at Arlington, and go home elated, with a bag full of appalling souvenirs and a new and innocent sort of pride. These highly organised parties pour like flood water down the marble corridors of the various temples. They are endearing and at present they wear Bermuda shorts and Madras cotton jackets – regardless of sex.

Or there is the other, hardly to be mentioned, Washington, which we, who live here, barely know. This is a raffish, hot, grease-smelling area which offers all the fun of the fair. It is not as wild as London or as exciting as New York. It is a curious little area of provincial vice close to the Union railroad station and within mortar shot of the Capitol. This was where the mayor of a last-ditch segregationalist town was taken by the old 'Murphy' game some weeks ago. He and some friends came to the city on political business. Requiring relaxation, they gave money to a stranger who promised entertainment. He never returned. The Negro – no stranger to the law – who did this became a sort of national hero for a few days.

You cannot encompass a city in a page of print. Washington is much more than this. Despite specialisation, it has become the epitome of the United States. Here is all the essential, man-sized smallness of this country and its almost accidental greatness. It is magnificent and it can be dreary. It is conservative and cautious and sophisticated and lacks eccentricity. It is a place where politics is talked in a manner that would be regarded as overdone at Westminster. It is no longer an alien place to Americans where people wear European clothes and forget about Springfield and Grand Rapids and Medicine Bend. It really is the capital. But, above all, just now, it is the place where *he* lives and which he dislikes.

The Observer, 15 August 1965

In 1962 he made his first visit to Poland and returned there in 1966.

Study of a unique country

Warsaw... To some in the West, Poland is a source of guilt, to others a possible weapon to be exploited against Moscow. To me, Poland is a nation interested mainly in survival, a nation, once famous for mad gestures and the elegant approach to death, now conducting as severely practical a policy as any in history. The interest and excitement of Poland are much more than that, of course. Poland is of the West in culture and spirit, and yet is an inherent part of the Eastern bloc. It is a living image of ourselves, caught up in the Communist apparatus. This works in us a special nervous curiosity.

Poland's external appearance is partly misleading. A tourist today could visit there without realising he was in a Communist country. There are almost no red stars, but a forest of crosses. There are no vast pictures of cold-eyed leaders, but a multitude of gesticulating saints. In Warsaw itself, the regime has thought it prudent to allow the Poles, still struggling to recover from their unimaginable war, to undertake one of the most gigantic acts of romanticism in history. The Poles have exquisitely restored the churches, palaces, streets and squares of the old part of their capital city. Whole districts look as if they have been untouched, not only by war but by time itself. The churches throughout the country are filled and services are attended with a fervour that we have never had to know. Sermons are long and serious. The priests walk in the streets in their soutanes and the nuns in their habits.

People speak almost, but not quite, as freely as in a free country. Nor is life any longer intolerable. There is still a des-

perate shortage of housing; living space is rationed on the basis
of size of family and the sort of work done. But since no one
can remember luxury, the longing for it has withered. Even
among the formerly rich, there is no longing for the distant
past. Sentimentality is out. The new aristocrats are the intellectuals. There is of course a censorship, but most books are available and they maintain a close knowledge of the West. They
prodigiously admire the American novel. A stranger could
find Polish intellectuals as uninsular, liberal and, at heart, as
free as any in the world. The realisation that this degree of freedom exists under Communism comes as a shock.

It cannot be understood without an awareness of the Polish
October. This was in 1956 and began with the Poznan riots, in
which 53 people died. The riots did not spread, but they
started a revolution inside the Party – the only place where it
could be effective. This grew into a Communist-nationalist
revolution headed by the old Party hero, Gomulka. In an
attempt to check this apparent danger, Khrushchev flew in
from Moscow. He was met by the blank wall of Gomulka's
firm but loyal opposition. The episode ended with an extraordinary understanding between Khrushchev and Gomulka,
so that Poland became reasonably free in her domestic arrangements.

The Polish October altered the Government's character, but
power remained finally with the Party. But by Communist
standards, it is an odd party. It offers a bare minimum of Marx-
ist doctrine. Resignation from it is permitted without punishment. It claims to be in transition. The class struggle, for
example, has been virtually abandoned; but belief in the eventual triumph of Communism is maintained. It is impossible to predict how Poland will develop; but, if peace holds, it
seems likely that Polish political, economic and religious doc-
trines will grow curiously blurred.

There are already two major anomalies in Polish life. The
first is agriculture. In Poland, the land has never been fully
nationalised. Before 1956, some 10,000 collective farms were
started. They were startlingly inefficient and have crumbled
away to 1,800. Poland today has a frankly peasant agriculture.
The average farm is of five hectares (12½ acres). And because
of a surviving Napoleonic law all farmers' sons must inherit or
be compensated. Yet the fact remains that Polish agriculture is

probably the most productive of any within the Socialist bloc today. The Government has accepted that the compelled peasant will not work. So most Polish land is a quilt of narrow fields marked with jealously white-washed boundary stones. Old women take a cow or geese to graze by the roadside or between fields. Wooden carts creak with fresh vegetables to the market. It is a profoundly conservative picture.

The other major anomaly is the Church. Poland remains a devoutly Catholic country and the Government is committed to changing this. But because of the obvious strength of the national attachment to Rome, they proceed with caution. Government officials actively dislike discussing this subject: they say they prefer talking of something more 'important'. On the surface, there is a mutual toleration. The Church is not actively persecuted. But the Government plays a strict and coldly legalistic role, enforcing the letter of the law on property, education and taxation – which usually works out to the disadvantage of the Church – and punishing the Church proselytisation as an infringement of the citizen's right to a free conscience. In the end both sides know the rules. The Poles will continue to flock to Our Lady of Czestochowa and to fill their churches. To attempt to break this loyalty would be to court such massive social disorder as to invite the Soviet intervention that both sides know would probably mean the final extinction of the Polish national identity. They would become just another Ukraine. The Church and the Communist Party are two inimical families condemned to live in the same house. But as long as the new pragmatism survives, the final catastrophe can be avoided. In the end, you come away admiring their acceptance of this reality just as if it had been a bold and heroic action in the old Polish tradition.

Poland suffered more from, and got less out of, the last war than any other nation. Yet only one old man in a Warsaw post office came up to me, an obvious foreigner, with an air of despair. They were slaves, he said, and he wanted nothing more than to leave Poland. I heard no one else speak in such a way. Most Poles do not seem to feel desperate. Moreover, they are not simply resigned to enduring a Socialist economy. In a country that was so utterly devastated and so little helped, State capitalism has seemed to most of them the only way to make a fresh start. When there is so little to go round, State planning is more emotionally tolerable than the hurly-burly of capitalism. If Poland were magically 'liberated' tomorrow, there would be Te Deums in the churches and someone different in government, but probably little fundamental change in the economic organisation of the State.

Again, although there is no entirely free discussion in Poland, it is probably true to say that the majority of Poles in Poland genuinely believe that the danger of war comes mainly from the West. Western policies are, they think, too often informed by a sort of careless evil. This attitude is based on an awareness of the fragility of their own situation. Under the Potsdam agreement of 1945, the Poles were given Upper and Lower Silesia, Pomerania and East Prussia, German lands since many centuries, as compensation for the loss to the Soviet Union of a roughly equivalent area of land. Over a period of two years, train-loads of Poles from the territories lost in the East moved in. The only alternative for these Polish migrants was to stay where they were and become Russian. Their transfer began in despair. Many of the new arrivals refused to unpack and waited resignedly for another enforced move. But, today, the settlement of these territories can be seen as remotely comparable with the story of modern Israel. It required a comparable team effort. And it has left the Poles with some equally resentful neighbours. Nevertheless, they have succeeded and have produced in one generation a young and integrated community in these lands.

The determination to keep these territories is unanimous in Poland. The Cardinal Primate Wyszynski, before his imprisonment by the Communists, established a Polish episcopate – and no nonsense about Vicars Apostolic – in the Recovered Territories. All Poles believe they have at last achieved logical frontiers. Yet every fundamental political argument in Poland ends with the fear of Germany, expressed or implied, and the horrors of the Second World War. They despise and try to ignore the docile, displaced East Germans. They hate and fear the Federal Republic. This attitude may be a rationalisation of their situation and their anxiety may be exaggerated. But in Poland it is as real as childbirth and as serious as death.

The Poles believe that the West, for its own convenience, has based its policy on support of West Germany; that West Germany has been armed irresponsibly; and that the West cannot ultimately control the Germans, particularly if they get nuclear weapons. They find sinister confirmation of their mistrust in our refusal to recognise as legitimate and final Poland's new frontier with East Germany. They therefore dread an eventual German revenge. In this situation Russia, instead of being the traditional enemy, becomes their only guarantee of survival. They accept this position with cold realism. A visiting journalist will often be asked not to emphasise the differences between Poland and the rest of the bloc, not to make Poland look too conspicuous. They want to fit in with what they have got. They are no longer high-spirited in their approach to foreign affairs. Instead, they take a clinical view of their position. Their diagnosis is as unemotional as that of a surgeon refusing to operate. Poland is today a vast national conspiracy, unplanned and unspoken, whose fated purpose must be not to embarrass its Communist Government too much.

The Observer, 2 September 1962

Celebrating a millennium

Poland has celebrated her millennium and there is obvious relief here that it is over without incident.

On 1 May, Labour Day, there was the usual vast and interminable Government-sponsored procession. Forests of red flags, pictures of Marx, rivers of enchanting children flowing past the tribune in front of the Palace of Culture. Young people were costumed to represent Polish history. Orchestras marched, playing against the loudspeakers. Factories, newspapers, universities, ministries, schools, the railways, all were represented: men with medals won out of the appalling experiences of this country, a few of them British, moved past, pleasantly happy, smiling and waving. The affair has become a sort of folk ritual that ambassadors and such must endure. It has an innocence, like an American parade. Mr. Gomulka briefly denounced the Americans as brutal aggressors and the American Embassy interpreted his speech as 'mild'. The Chinese looked ostentatiously bored.

Two days later the Catholics held *their* celebration, 200

kilometres away at Czestochowa. This was different. The country had been filled with rumours of the difficulties that would be set in the way of pilgrims. No foreign delegations and few journalists were allowed there. There were tales of police blocks, of possible arrest, of no trains, no accommodation, no buses. Some cars were stopped by police eight times on the way from Warsaw. The police were ruefully courteous. Yet, as a result, the crowds at the shrine were less than the unimaginable concourse that had been expected. Some 300,000 only gathered in front of the battlements.

Czestochowa is a dreary industrial city. On a hill above it stands a Vaubanesque castle. Within it is a monastery with two churches. A tall, elegiac tower drifts up towards the sky, streaming with banners. On the main battlement, they had built a huge altar with the Polish eagle on it. On each side there was a throne, one for the Pope left spectacularly empty, and one for the Cardinal, spectacularly filled. A brass band in white surplices tootled a salute at every great moment. Long flights of stairs were crowded with clergy. It was a setting for an extreme baroque drama. Below it were the sloping meadows covered with people of all sorts, all staring up at the ceremonial on the battlements. Here, in the seventeenth century, the great Swedish advance was turned back. It is said and occasionally believed that the Swedes were finally defeated by the display of an ikon. The face of the Virgin of Czestochowa, dark, impersonal, almost threatening, bears slashes said to have been made with a Swedish sword. This is the talisman of Poland.

The picture was taken down from its setting above the altar and carried round the battlements. People knelt at the sight of it. It was borne in turn by priests, doctors, nurses, miners, writers, farmworkers and journalists and finally back to the altar by bishops. It came lurching along in its heavy silver case, covered with jewels, an almost terrible spectacle. The great Polish hymns, that seem to celebrate Poland as much as the Mother of God, rolled up from the crowd below. One of the most tremendous was composed in the eighteenth century during the partition of Poland. It contained the line, 'Give us back our free fatherland.' In 1918 this was officially changed to 'Bless, O Lord, our free fatherland.' The crowd, without premeditation, sang the older version. Then the cardinal covered the picture with a new set of jewels. This is the third time in history this has been done. Both previous sets were the gifts of the Popes. Now, it was proudly announced, it was time for Polish jewels.

The cardinal had been made the Papal Legate for the occasion, and a bishop said: 'Those who wanted to deprive us of the presence of the Pope have lost, because the Pope is present in your person.' Applause was frantic. Another said the Pope did not come because God did not require it. There was little political comment, but this was plainly a Polish act of triumph. The Government has been embarrassed and is still deeply angry with the cardinal. The cardinal is unrepentant.

The Observer, 8 May 1966

He preferred not to write about Ireland. It was difficult to be objective. But he did write, once, in 1964, about the town of his forefathers, and in 1969, after the eruption of the Northern Ireland Troubles, he wrote a potted history of the island.

Where I come from

*Clonakilty...*This little town has a certain, awkward fame. Irishmen in Ireland, on Third Avenue in New York, or in Coventry and Northwest London, tend to ejaculate 'God help us' after its name – and it is not a prayer.

Clonakilty is a small town in West Cork. It is not one of the treasures of Ireland. It was never an English garrison town – so it lacks the usual mall of elegant houses where the exiled officers lived and the stark ruins of a barracks that invariably marked the Irish reaction to their presence. It has none of the tragic and unrestored ruins that litter Ireland – the shells of abbeys, the broken towers of its various rulers, the burnt-out casings of Edwardian country houses, the great lumps of stonework, shrouded with ivy, the surviving corners of old castles, where this hero died or that host murdered his guest. It is unostentatious and of almost Macedonian bareness. It is a long street of small houses, painted in bright, surprising colours. There is a suggestion of horse dung about the streets. The windows are all blinded with lace. There is a monument, a statue of a man holding a pike in memory of one of their hopeless uprisings. There are hot little low-ceilinged, stout-scented bars with none of the homely splendours of the English pub, but bare, dark, undecorated, single-minded and each with the name of its owner exquisitely painted over its front.

There is the Protestant church, high on a hillside, lording it sadly over a bulging graveyard where Catholics and Protestants lie side by side in the only mutual peace they ever knew for any length of time. And theirs is now for ever. And in the centre of Clonakilty, spiky, unforgiving, wildly extravagant and greyly sad, is the Catholic church. It cost a packet in 1880. It was almost a gesture of defiance at a time when the town was run by a few richly-stomached Protestant families who alone held the keys of politics, office and admitted respectability. It is cathedral-sized. It is remorselessly Gothic. It glows with white marble and with granite the colour of brawn. It was built by the poor as a gesture of expected triumph. It glistens with cleanliness and varnish. Flour-white statues of the saints stand in every available niche. A hundred years of pastors lie buried at its entrance. It is Clonakilty's great gesture and there is a splendour about it in a place that was once poor, that impels admiration. The Presbyterian church is now the post office – there are no Presbyterians left. The Methodist church struggles to survive. The Church of Ireland on its grave-stuffed hill has a gentle, defeated air.

This is not a romantic place and no one grieves. If there is little new building, that is because there is still room in the houses emptied and emasculated by the terrible history of the place. But the paint is new. Tractors are replacing the horses, lorries the donkeys. Clonakilty has wormed its way quietly into the twentieth century. The television aerials are out. The small cars make gratifying traffic jams. The hotels are installing bathrooms and neon lighting. The church is as full as any railway station in the world. It is not quaint, or tragic or nice. This odd town is a monument to the second arrival of a people – the first was independence, the second the utilisation of what they had won. It has become, for the first time in its sad history, a good place to live in – but then I confess prejudice.

The Observer, May 1964

Short history of Ireland

The history of Ireland is vague. There was a neolithic culture which was invaded by Celts in the sixth century BC. They intermarried briskly. This period is also covered by a multitude of heroic legends which are more important than the facts. The first invaders came under a chief called Partolan. They all died of a plague. Then the Nemedians, who were defeated by the Fomorians. The Nemedians, who came from Scythia, retired to Greece and returned as Firbolgs. Then the tribe of the god Danu came from Greece. (These eventually retired into the hills and became fairies.) Finally from Scythia there were the Milesians. One of their kings, Niall of the Nine Hostages, set up his capital at Tara, and at the time of the Roman departure from Britain established colonies in West Wales.

Before the coming of Christianity, there were four confederate kingdoms, ruled by noble blood relations, and their titular head was the High King. There were three other principalities that did not recognise his primacy. The people were pantheists and fire-worshippers and believed in fairies. When St. Patrick came there was a considerable civilisation. They worked gold, codified their laws, revered poets as much as princes, had judges and verbal chroniclers and even a sort of general assembly. St. Patrick came in AD 432. His achievements have probably been proudly and lovingly exaggerated. Most of his work was in Ulster. (Ulster, in history, is the Celtic and political heartland of Ireland.) There had been a scattering of Christians before him with their own saints like Declan. Patrick established his See at Armagh. He knew the language, having previously been a slave in Ireland for seven years. He was tolerant of pagan customs and fashioned the new Irish faith in the discipline of Rome. It did not remain there.

The Irish developed a monastic culture in which the country was littered with religious settlements; rough huts around a rude oratory. An African village is the closest physical analogy. Sex was spurned, and yet these places became the repository of West Europe's culture. They cultivated Latin, even that of the classics. European scholars at a deadly time came to share their austerity and learning. They wrote enchanting poems about the beauty of Ireland and illuminated majestic holy books whose survivors are among Europe's treasures. They could not sit still, and their missionaries went to Scotland, England, Western Europe and Italy. This is regarded as that Golden Age which every nation is allowed once in its history. They recognised the primacy of Rome, but spent more time giving the Popes advice than obeying their orders. The abbots were supreme; the bishops were tribal figures whose job was to ordain. The monks shaved the front of their heads instead of using the Roman bald spot tonsure. They computed Easter in the Jewish manner.

But outside the monasteries from the fourth to the eighth centuries there were ceaseless tribal wars. In the eighth century the Norse raids began. These itinerant raiders settled permanently around Dublin. They were finally defeated by the High King, Brian Boru, at the battle of Clontarf in 1014. He was killed while saying his prayer for victory. (It was about this time that the O'Donovans were driven out of Clare for encompassing the death of his brother.)

In the twelfth century the anarchic state of the Church was reformed by St. Malachy, who died on his way to Rome in the arms of Bernard of Clairvaux. But in England, Henry II, the remote executioner of Becket, planned the conquest of Ireland. This project was approved by Pope Adrian IV. (He was born Nicholas Breakspear in Hertfordshire.) He wanted a tighter control over the saintly eccentricities of the Irish Church. Henry entrusted the invasion to the Lords of the Welsh Marches. The most famous of these was 'Strongbow', the Earl of Pembroke. And in 1169 the Anglo-Norman conquest of Ireland began. They conquered because of their unity and superior skill. In 1172 the Irish kings recognised Henry as their overlord.

War and killing were almost continuous. In 1367 the Statute of Kilkenny forbade intermarriage between the Normans and the Irish. But by the time of Henry VIII, the foreign barons were indistinguishable from the Irish. Henry took the title of King of Ireland. Edward VI began the introduction of Protestantism. Unlike the English Catholic collapse, very few bishops and priests took the Oath of Supremacy, and though Elizabeth avoided extreme religious harshness, the Irish began to understand that conforming to the English reformed religion meant the complete acceptance of English rule. It is a lesson they never forgot. Religion became the cohesive force where the tribal system had been divisive. It became the symbol and strength of their patriotism. There was a series of savage rebellions. There was a sort of Renaissance magnificence in the barbarities of the Queen's agents in Ireland as they put them down. But they were effective, both with poison at the table and in pitched battles. They destroyed in Munster an Irish-Spanish force at Kinsale. This led to wholesale expulsions and the granting of land to Englishmen like Spenser and Raleigh. In the north, Essex failed to contain them. Mountjoy (after whom a Dublin jail is named) did the job professionally, and many of the great Irish magnates fled the country. England now regarded the Irish as savages who kept the corrupt Faith and wanted friendship with Spain.

James I began the major Plantation of Ulster. Scots and English (mainly Presbyterian) artisans and farmers were settled on the lands of the Northern Earls. In 1641 there was yet another rebellion of the old and the Norman Irish in which a large number of Protestants were killed. This was crushed by Cromwell and Ireton with a series of even more spectacular massacres whose memory lingers in Ireland as 'the curse of Cromwell'. Every priest met with was automatically killed. Landowners of both sorts were banished west of the Shannon 'to Hell or Connaught' and their estates given to soldiers and London merchants. Some believe that this displaced and destitute aristocracy survives in the itinerant tinkers.

In 1688 Catholics rose for the Stuarts, who never did anything for Ireland. This is when they besieged the Protestants in Derry. It was an heroic siege in which the defendants ate rats and candles and the apprentices shut the gates when the mayor wished to capitulate. William ('King Billy') defeated James II at the Battle of the Boyne and, in the end, the surviving Catholic leaders fled to the Continent ('The Wild Geese'). Some of them and their descendants formed regiments for the French. ('We had the honour at Fontenoy to beat the Guards Brigade.') Some of their descendants became Marshals in the armies of Austria and Napoleon.

Ireland was now in the control of largely absentee landlords, and all its native leaders gone. Catholics were under the Penal Code. They had no rights of citizenship and few of ownership. The land was in the hands of the Protestant oligarchy. And the

Presbyterians of Ulster still sometimes made common cause with the Irish against the Anglicans' supremacy. When the American War of Independence began in 1776, much of the army was withdrawn, and to keep them quiet the Irish were given a Parliament, albeit a Protestant one. It sat in what is now the Bank of Ireland in Dublin. It spoke for Ireland none the less. It was dominated by Henry Grattan.

In 1798 there was a futile French revolutionary invasion at Bantry Bay and a rising of the poor; some of its leaders were parish clergy. It was crushed and punished in the traditional way. Pitt, tired of the Dublin Parliament, distrusted its semi-independence, and by bribery and a liberal distribution of titles (which survive on the visiting cards of Britain's most cultivated and civilised lordlings), got the Parliament to abolish itself, and in 1801 the Act of Union became law. There were to be 28 Irish peers elected by themselves in the House of Lords. This could be done tomorrow again if only there were an Irish Lord Chancellor still to summon them to an election. There were also to be four bishops in the Lords and 100 members in the Commons. All Protestants: no Catholics got into the Commons until 1829.

Now the state of Ireland was the scandal of Europe. The peasantry was nearly illiterate. They lived on potatoes and learned to please their masters. They went to school in hedges and heard Mass in secret places. The potatoes needed only a few months' work a year to cultivate, and, for the rest, they sat and talked in miserable huts and occasionally distilled liquor. The language and the spoken poetry survived. They were brutalised and reduced by honourable men in much the same way that Hitler intended to treat the Slavs. The small Anglo-Irish ascendancy became a brilliant minority, 'horse Protestants', true, and often cruelly exploitive landlords, but also the progenitors of the best of what was known as Irish poetry and plays. And many, like Parnell, were dedicated Irish patriots. Upon this miserable society, the potato famine of 1846 came like a plague to Egypt, and the Irish diaspora became a flood. By death and departure, the population was halved.

Ireland changed from tillage to pasture and the land hunger of peasants became an overriding political fact, frequently expressed in anti-landlord violence. In 1886 Gladstone began his frustrating fight for Home Rule, while the Irish Party under

Parnell brought Parliament almost to a stop. Parnell himself was destroyed in his prime by the Irish because of his honest adultery. In 1914 Asquith's Bill for Home Rule received the Royal Assent, but was shelved because of the Great War in which the Irish fought like the English. ('More Irishmen died fighting for England than for Ireland.') But Ulster, once the most Irish part of Ireland, had changed. The Protestants were appalled at the prospect of domination by the Catholic majority, and under Carson were prepared to take up rebellious arms in defence of the British connection. The British Army connived. Again the war shelved that action. During the war the Easter Rising distracted the British at a bad time in 1916. That too was suppressed, with many British casualties, and the leaders (less De Valera) were executed. Their deaths united Catholic Ireland.

After the war there was a vicious guerrilla war between the British and Irish underground. The British imported ex-Service irregulars, the Black and Tans, whose reputation is the worst of any British formation in history. To staunch the intolerable and unclosable wound, Lloyd George entered into negotiations with the Irish leaders. A group of schoolmasters, underground soldiers and poets came to London. They faced the most formidable Cabinet team ever fielded for Britain. De Valera did not attend.

Tricked and bullied, in 1921 the Irish delegation signed a maimed (from the Irish point of view) Treaty. Michael Collins in signing said it was his death warrant. De Valera, the president of the non-existent republic, repudiated it and Ireland sank into a civil war in which those who accepted the treaty fought those who rejected it. Michael Collins died in ambush at Irish hands. The scars of that war still disfigure the Republic of Ireland and dominate her politics. Her two main parties are still derived from those who accepted or rejected the treaty. The treaty did not include Ulster. A Boundary Commission drew a frontier for the Province that was to stay British. A South African judge on the Commission resigned in disgust. The Six Counties – Antrim, Armagh, Derry, Fermanagh and Tyrone – stayed put and acquired a Government subject to Westminster and controlled by an exclusive Protestant society, the Orange Order. The Free State (as it was known then) began its journey towards sovereignty. In the South the Border became a sacred issue that only recently was being quietly shelved as an irrelevance to the business of building a prosperous, sober, almost Scandinavian little republic. And yet the existence of the border was made by De Valera the excuse for his neutrality in the Second World War, which cost the lives of many English sailors and soldiers. And no voice in Ireland was raised against this policy, despite the fact that more southern Irishmen served against Germany than Irishmen from the North. But in the North they have dedicated themselves, the Protestants, to survival under the fiscal generosity of the Union Jack. But it is not a selfish reaction. It is a genuine ideological hold-up.

They are all Irish. All cursed by their history. And they are still working out the destiny ordained by one of the most tragic of national stories. For this, under God, the English must bear the blame. It is the worst thing a gentle people has ever done to another.

The Observer, 24 August 1969

Poster designed by Hans Unger and displayed in London underground stations to advertise Patrick O'Donovan's *Inside America* column.

October 1958

Top left: Patrick O'Donovan on his last day as a Major in the Irish Guards, Tournai, 4 April 1946.

Top right: Patrick O'Donovan, wearing his Irish Guards service cap, reporting on the Korean War from Seoul in 1953.

Above: Patrick O'Donovan (right) on his first assignment to Jerusalem as a Foreign Correspondent in June 1948 with two officers from the Second Battalion Grenadier Guards.

Top left: Hermione Fitzherbert-Brockholes at the time of her marriage to Patrick O'Donovan in September 1954.

Top right: Taken for Patrick O'Donovan's *Cachet du Service de Presse* in 1960 while he was covering the war in the Congo for *The Observer*.

Above: Ballyluck, Ardfield, Clonakilty, West Cork, Ireland, home of Patrick O'Donovan's ancestors.

Above left: Practising Irish ballads with Conor Cruise O'Brien in Washington, 1959.

Above right: Discussing world affairs in 1965. Patrick O'Donovan with Max Jakobson, Finnish Ambassador to the United Nations.

Right: Leaving to report on floods in Chile in June 1960, wearing a coat loaned for the occasion by David Astor, then editor of *The Observer*.

The Gold Coast in February 1951: 'A door in the white wall of Fort James was opened at 1.15 p.m. today in Accra and the British Administration released Kwame Nkrumah...' Patrick and other British correspondents were there to greet him.

Holding a Press Conference at the University of California at Los Angeles, after receiving for the second time the University's Foreign Press Award for 'distinguished reporting of many important phases of the American scene', 1960.

Consulting with colleagues at the United Nations in 1965.

Patrick O'Donovan with David Astor (centre left) and Marcus, now Lord, Sieff (left) in the early 1960s.

Patrick O'Donovan on his first visit to Warsaw in 1962.

Above Being introduced to Pope Paul VI in 1970 before undertaking the translation of the Latin text of the Pontifical Commission's 'Pastoral Instruction on Social Communication' for the English-speaking world.

Right: With the Chaplains of the Royal Irish Rangers, Berlin 1980.

The Patrick O'Donovan familiar to Alresford in his later years, photographed by Jane Bown, his favourite colleague on assignment.

Part Two

BIOGRAPHICAL NOTE 1967–1981

As Patrick's health deteriorated and travel became the exception and, perforce, his interests more parochial, he was offered a weekly column in *The Catholic Herald*. In January 1976 he took over the Charterhouse Chronicle (*The Catholic Herald's* office was then in Charterhouse Street) and gradually built up an amused and loyal readership, while still on the staff of *The Observer*, to which he was attached by an umbilical cord which only they could have severed. Exceptionally well informed for a layman, totally fascinated by Christianity in general but his own faith in particular, preferring the company of prelates to any other and the vicissitudes of the Church to world affairs, Patrick for the first time began to write as if in a letter to close friends and, as it were, slowly prepared himself in print for the death he knew could not be long postponed. He wrote of his friends: David Astor, his editor and mentor; Father D'Arcy, whom he'd known since Oxford, whose life he'd saved in Tokyo, who had married him; Douglas Woodruff who had steered him into endless and financially unrewarding evenings of lecturing by advising him that it was his duty to use his talents for the Church; Nico Henderson, who became our Ambassador in Washington and who had been instrumental in his joining *The Observer* in the first place. Surprisingly insecure, it was only when he was sure that it would cost *The Observer* more to sack him and make a redundancy payment than to continue paying his salary until his retirement did he relax and cease to fear that he was on the point of dismissal.

In February 1981, while staying at the Cumberland Hotel in London to work on the script for a series of BBC programmes on Germany immediately after the Second World War, he had his first appalling haemorrhage and was from then on almost constantly in hospital. On 25 October *The Observer* printed his last contribution, a speculation on the wisdom of the proposed

Papal visit to this country. His last Charterhouse Chronicle mourned the death of a friend – and obliquely his own. But the last thing he wrote – dictated to his wife as she lay beside him, herself barely recovered from an operation for a spinal tumour – was an article he had promised for the Anglican parish magazine; it was about a birth, about Christmas. Always reliable and professional, Patrick left behind him no work unfinished and his affairs in perfect order.

He died on Wednesday 23 December 1981.

Home Thoughts

Virtue on a vast scale

The Royal Northern is not one of the famous hospitals of London with reputations as great as royally-chartered universities. It is anonymous, on the outside gaunt-windowed, raw-bricked, lost in the faded Pooter elegance of the back streets of Holloway. I was sent there because, in a hurry, the doctor found an empty bed. I have no regrets. It can take 300 persons and for a few weeks I have been one of them, a subject of a superb organisation that uses an almost military technique to ends that command the admiration of people who must live and die a little frightened. Such gaunt institutions, built for the most part at a bad time in British building, are suppressed in most people's consciousness. And yet, if it were necessary, and as a Christian, I would grind every cathedral in the country to powder to keep them going. It is the nurses that summon up resources of admiration I never knew I had. There is a conventional attitude to this rank of women. Old men will knuckle their foreheads and say 'God bless you, Miss.' Taxi drivers will cut their fares. Police will never make trouble for them. They can travel first class on third class tickets. A rustle of starch and a curious lacy *vol-au-vent* perched on a female head, and the hard turn soft and the fierce gentle. No such respect is given to doctors or clerics. Part of this respect comes from the guilt of knowing that nurses are underpaid, overworked, disciplined as Guardsmen, and do things that are unmentionable and which, increasingly, the family will no longer do for itself.

There are complaints, of course, of women doing the right things for the wrong reasons, of female ward Caesars, even of casual cruelty. But for a few weeks I have been at their mercy, and if this is the season of temporary good will, then the nurses have all of mine. Clearly they are the most spectacular stream that pours from that great reservoir of human goodness which is women. Their job is an essentially womanly one, but not really a motherly one. There is no definable nursing type. Some are like members of a Victorian royal family. Some are enchanting flibberty-gibbets who probably live it up on gin and lime on their days off. Some sail up to one's bed and drop anchor like great galleons.

Some are so sceptical about one's pain that the pain stops out of shame. Some are simply serene young women doing a job that dignifies the whole human race. And they come from so many countries that at times one had the illusion that all the ex-colonies were gathered in cool kindness around the sick bed of the Empire. But the discipline is still there, less stringent than when a nurse was not allowed to look Matron in the face. And it offends some people, because they detest all discipline: they cannot see why they should be called at dawn, why there should be rules about fags and booze, why families should not be allowed to spend all day at the bedside. There are some in hospital who are so disturbed that they would resent the suggestion that they blow their own nose. And there are some who treat the nursing staff like servants – when in fact they are highly trained and charged with a responsibility in sudden emergency that can give them, briefly, the authority of a doctor. And of course there are times when things go wrong and the authority distorts the woman, and the patient suffers helplessly.

But, essentially, these nurses are bringing order into a disorderly situation. Illness can be an insult and a degradation. Pain can reduce a man to the level of an animal creeping into a corner. Nurses practise the sort of naval discipline that is fundamentally reasonable and which is designed to sustain humans faced with horror and filth and inhumanity. They have, like sailors, to face an unnatural situation and love itself is insufficient in such a predicament. The climax of all this traditional order comes at an operation. Now there are various cunning drugs that can send a man to the knife smiling slightly and devoid of curiosity and fear. There are currently complaints about operating theatres. I never saw mine, but was gently switched off by a little green gnome who was probably the anaesthetist. And all around was this controlled and unhurried discipline, no barked orders, no panic, no sense of crisis. As long as I was conscious someone told me all the time what was happening. Someone gave the right degree of believable reassurance. Someone touched me with just the right sort of unsentimental and affectionate respect for a body in a vile predicament.

Of course they have seen it all before. I think the disgusting details still disgust them, but they have their disgust under control. Their attention to me rightly diminished as my needs got smaller. They did not lose their dignity or femininity in the face of the gross and helpless nudity of the sick. They were never impersonal. I would like to step out of the ritual objectivity that is imposed, at least in theory, upon a reporter, and salute this regiment of women. They will be extremely surprised and a little suspicious about my motives. But it is possible, occasionally, to stop being cynical and to salute virtue on a vast and organised scale, and this I now do.

The Observer, 24 December 1967

With travelling rarely possible, Patrick wrote 'of cabbages and kings' for The Observer *and, for* The Catholic Herald, *the weekly Charterhouse Chronicle.*

In the Canterbury manner

The enthronement of the Most Reverend Father-in-God, Donald, Lord Archbishop of Canterbury and Primate of All England, was astonishing. For certain the 101st Archbishop, a man known for plain living, no nonsense and sound Biblical scholarship, had the most splendid installation in the whole history of the office.

The enthronement is one of those ceremonies that are revered in England. The coronation of a monarch is the greatest of them. And in medieval England the King would 'wear' his crown at least three times a year in different cities to make his status plain and public. So with the Archbishop. Then the word would get around among the illiterate that a new man, Becket, for instance, had been seen wearing the pallium and blessing the people.

Enthronement is basically a legal act, with the admission of the new Archbishop by the Chapter, who are guardians of the

See, the reading of the legal mandate from the Royal Commissioners, and the taking of the oath on a book of the Gospels kept at Corpus Christi, in Cambridge, which may be the one Pope Gregory gave to Augustine, the first incumbent of this See. Dr. Coggan was, of course, already a bishop, so there was no call to consecrate him. But the physical and legal taking over of his See was made into an act of prayer. In the seventeenth and eighteenth centuries the ceremony was unregarded and almost private. It is only in this century that it has been clothed in steadily increasing splendour.

Such ceremonies are symbolic statements, and this was a most emphatic statement of intent by the new Archbishop, who had the last word in all the arrangements. The claims of Christianity to an essential place within society and the State were made more plainly and powerfully by deed than they could be by word. So the whole visible apparatus of British and local power was there. It is true that the trade unions, the merchant banks and the Stock Exchange were not there officially. Instead there was a dazzling display of what traditionally passes for authority. There were the heads of universities in rich gowns. There were rows of well-furred counsellors, gold chains and swords carried like upside-down crosses. There was some of the Cabinet and leaders of political parties. There were the Speaker and the Lord Chancellor in breeches and fine silk stockings, despite wigs and encrusted gowns, spoiled visually for ever by Gilbert and Sullivan's irreverence. And there was a part of the Royal Family, professionally at home and at ease.

But the ceremony was also an unprecedentedly bold assertion of the basic unity of Christians. So there were Copts in black turbans, Armenians in silk pixie hoods, Russian and Greek prelates looking, as always, just a little aloof, nothing uncivil, mind you, but conducting themselves as if they still had certain reservations. But it was the Romans who were the most surprising. At the Coronation of George VI the Pope's representative sat out the ceremony in the porch of Westminster Abbey and special allowances had to be made for the Duke of Norfolk, a Catholic, to carry out his duties as Earl Marshal. On this occasion three cardinals attended, a sudden blindingly scarlet, utterly counter-Reformation explosion in the course of the procession.

There were the Archbishops of Paris and Brussels Malines,

both determined and powerful liberals within the ecclesiastical spectrum. There was Cardinal Willebrands, who is a sound Dutchman and Head of the Secretariat for Christian Unity in the Vatican. The Pope's representative in Britain, the Apostolic Delegate, Archbishop Heim, who lives in Wimbledon, but does not rate diplomatic status, walked in purple with the cardinal. They could not help looking apart. Their faces seemed drawn and austere among the Anglican donnish cast of countenance which prevailed around them. They sang, too, as they walked up the aisle and then crouched comfortably in their monastic stalls as if sitting out a familiar office. In fact, nine cardinals have held Canterbury. The last was Reginald Pole, a wise and moderate man, who for a time was considered a possible Pope. He had the good fortune to die the day before Mary Tudor.

But then, this See did not really require a red hat. It always had an almost patriarchal dignity, if only because it was so far from Rome, so physically detached, and because after smashing the pretensions of York, it played almost always a towering role within the Government of the State. This role, a little late, maybe, was re-asserted now as never before. As always, the English performed as if they were born to ceremonial and never had to rehearse. The diverse processions shunted effortlessly into place. No masters of ceremonies bustled, hissing instructions and clicking their fingers. No choirboy misbehaved. It was a bit triumphant at a time of apparent defeat, but then that is a very proper condition for an act of prayer.

The Observer, 26 January 1975

Cardinal in changing times

John Carmel Heenan, the Cardinal Archbishop of Westminster who died on Friday, came to his see in a resounding flurry of pomp and publicity. In England, few bishops of any sect have ever had so great a welcome. There was a sort of joy at his coming, and not only among English Catholics. The British press greeted him as a new and exciting national figure. That was back in 1963, in another ecclesiastical era. The English

Catholics, unlike their Irish brethren, have no primate. But Westminster has a vast Victorian Byzantine cathedral which is a masterpiece of its time, clad in rare marbles, where the liturgy is celebrated as magnificently as anywhere in the world, and its holder invariably gets a cardinal's hat while in office.

Dr. Heenan, for he was both a doctor of divinity and of philosophy, had been transferred from the see of Liverpool. He came with a powerful reputation as a speaker and a broadcaster, as a friend of the press, as a man of strong personality and strong views. He succeeded a series of safe and, if the truth be told, rather uninteresting cardinal archbishops who had been good canon lawyers. They were men who had kept the exclusivity of the faith, men who expected and got an almost unquestioning obedience from priests and people, but were intellectually rather middle-class princes of the Church. Dr. Heenan seemed to promise a wonderful renewal, an access of new confidence and a fierce activity that would not respect either custom or personalities in its zeal for the welfare of Christianity. He has undoubtedly been one of the great archbishops of Westminster.

But then, in September 1964, the Second Vatican Council met in Rome, summoned on the sudden whim of Pope John. It was one of the most important Councils in the history of the Church, and there are plenty of good Catholics who will say it was one of the most disastrous. It did – to generalise – several things. It admitted that the Church had acted sinfully at times in history. It preached a new, almost revolutionary tolerance. It eroded, unintentionally, the authority of the Pope and the bishops. It seemed to diminish the ancient exclusivity of the Roman Church.

It may have been good Christianity. It was certainly bad politics. For it seemed to make it easier to leave the Church and less urgent to join her. Conscience now sat on the throne beside authority, and the most obvious public results of the Council were the resignation of many priests from their office, a falling off in vocations and conversions, and a new sort of doubt about the validity of some of the Church's commands, especially those about birth control.

Heenan played a considerable role in the Council, speaking reasonably and in Latin on the liberal side, standing for an

English sort of moderation and gradual reform. In 1965 he was made a cardinal and he had, in England, to bear the brunt of the changes, good and bad, that came out of that Council. But as the results of the Vatican Council became more obvious, there were times when the office must have been actively painful to him. Distinguished priests defied him and left the Church. The criticisms from inside the family are often uncharitable, and no serious pastor can fail to grieve over his slowly dwindling flock.

So his pastorate that began so joyously had not been easy. Had he been a politician he might by then have had a broken heart. He had the advantage of being a priest, and he was a man who did his remarkable best and left the rest to God.

The Observer, November 1975

Father D'Arcy

For most educated men in Britain, Father D'Arcy, who died last week, was the epitome of all that was brilliant or dangerous within the Roman Church, of all that was sensitive or guileful among the Jesuits. In fact he was as representative of his time as any poet, politician or journalist.

Martin D'Arcy was a tiny man, very delicate to look at, bird-boned and beak-nosed, with a prematurely fashionable bush of hair, and darting eyes. He looked as impermanent as a twig stuck in sand. He was actually as tough as a fine piece of miniature engineering. His manners were exquisite. He dressed fastidiously – not for him the clerical soup stain. His appearance was so striking that he was painted and photographed as often as are minor royalty. He was used as an archetype in novels and was the original of Father Rothschild in Evelyn Waugh's book *Vile Bodies*. People went to extravagant lengths to meet him.

The lives of priests, unless they are on the run, caught and executed, make thin biography. Their drama is usually internal. Father D'Arcy's life, despite the fact that he never sought publicity, seemed to have been lived very publicly, surrounded by distinguished friends, and all his geese, some of them exceedingly odd, were swans to him. He was born in Bath in 1888, the son of a barrister whose family came from Co. Roscommon. He went to school with the Jesuits at Stoneyhurst and then pursued that long course of training and teaching that made him a priest and finally, in 1933, the Master of Campion Hall at Oxford. He acquired some old students' lodgings and got Sir Edwin Lutyens to build a small, handsome and solid hall there which became an integral and admired part of the University. There he entertained both distinguished and undergraduate visitors as well as supervising his own intense Jesuit students. He did both with a sort of happy ease. He also began the collection of beautiful and strange things that became almost an embarrassment to the Society of Jesus, which only really cares for such things as practical aids to religion. Pictures, statues, chalices, vestments, crucifixes, all presents from friends. He also acquired a most rare collection of Stuart portraits. He did indeed love beautiful things, but there was a pleasant kindness in the acquisivity. He was trying to get back ancient objects to their original use and parallel to this was a sentimental weakness for noble families. Both were part of his conservative reverence for continuity.

He visited the United States during the war. Naturally it was said that he went as an agent of the British Government to win round the Catholic community there who, at the start, tended to be lamentably isolationist. He was lecturing at a Jesuit university. On one feast day evening they put on the British documentary, 'Desert Victory.' The young Jesuits barracked. He walked out. He refused to speak to anyone except on religion or his lectures. It worked. A deputation came at last with a courteous apology.

In 1945 he was made Provincial, that is the Superior, of the Jesuits in England. This was a mistake. He was not at ease either with Roman authority or with financial affairs and he had a tendency to buy country houses for the Society that had more aesthetic or historical justification than practical use. So his term ended in some unhappiness. None the less, the Society gave him a complete and loving freedom to lecture, travel and write. In fact his books were curiously opaque for so lucid a teacher and talker. I have heard him sadly mourn his failure as a creative theologian or historian and do it with a sad and terrible sincerity. But his fame and his friendships were not based on his writings. They lay in his flashing personality, in his ability to inspire affection and admiration. His great and indefinable achievement was, without proselytising, to give new life to the idea that a contempt for institutional religion and the swift dismissal of the idea of God were neither brave nor chic, nor necessarily right. His influence was enormous and accounted for shoals of converts, which included Evelyn Waugh and Dame Edith Sitwell.

His great days ended with the Second Vatican Council. The Church changed. He could not comprehend the priestly defectors. He lacked the will or the youth to change. He grieved over the innovations. He never prayed publicly but in Latin. He did not complain nor allow himself any sort of disloyalty to authority. Some of his gaiety was replaced by sadness. He waited for death, not as a release, but as the most natural thing in the world. *The Observer, 28 November 1976*

Consorting with the gentry

The Game Fair must be one of the oddest festivals in Britain. It is a two-day affair and it happens every year in the demesne of some great house. This year it was at the Duke of Wellington's place at Stratfield Saye, in Hampshire. He has a vast and exquisitely barbered park, very open, with carefully placed clumps of enormous trees, and the river Loddon and an artificial lake. The fair is devoted to the killing of wild things – usually, it seems, for their own good – by methods that are formal, difficult, and, if death were the only purpose of the operation, manifestly inefficient. But all this appertains to a life style and the sporting side of it; the careful preservation and the ritual killing are its liturgy and symbolism and joy.

The people were among the most interesting of the exhibits. Some had come from far away. All made the effort to look landed, except the farm labourers, who tended to have long hair and very fancy trousers, and the gamekeepers, who seemed to ignore the occasional sun and the heavy humidity in a tightly buttoned, tweedy, Edwardian formality. The gentry carefully dressed down in an expensive way. There were

women in ageless and sexless hats carrying on animated con-
versations. They tended to tow passive dogs, which now and
again they would address in terms of almost hysterical rage,
ordering them to 'sit', or something. And of course there were
the piercing voices of imperious children.

There were endless demonstrations and competitions going
on so far apart that you had to be a countryman to survive the
walking. Young men banged away all day at clay pigeons.
There was a Scotsman in a kilt doing remarkable things with a
rod and line as he whipped it backwards and forwards to drop
a fly far away and exactly in place on the water. There was
archery, there were dog trials, and horses, though I do not
know if foxes count as vermin or game. There were hawks
which were lovely and terrible to look at, the personification of
small menace. And when I was there there was a pretty and
intelligent girl who lured a hawk-eagle out of a high tree. He
had been scared by the prevalence of dogs, and she whirled a
lure round her head until he came down and was rewarded
with a gobbet of red meat.

Around these essentials was the great rural trade fair that
sold rather depressing sporting art, fantastic Welsh woollen
clothes, food for domestic pets, lordly estate agents dispensing
drink, where you could have picked up an estate for yourself,
country crafts that looked as if they had a small back-up
factory near Birmingham, 'indestructible socks', every sort of
sporting equipment, bars, buffets, ecology, forestry, water
conservancy, more than you could see in a day.

On Friday the Duke of Wellington's house was open to the
public for the first time. It stands well apart, long, low, pleasantly undistinguished, at the heart of this marvellous fair. Its
core was started in 1630, but it has been greatly changed. The
great Duke bought it and the estate in 1817 out of the £600,000
voted him by Parliament for the provision of a suitable country
seat. In fact, he planned to pull it down and build a palace to
rival Blenheim. He was a man who listened to advice as well
as giving it. Having heard his financial advisers, he merely
enlarged the house a little. It is a curiously moving place. The
corridors are narrow, the rooms small. The long gallery is
almost pokey. The dining room is intimate. The upper rooms
are closed to the public. He liked pasting prints directly on to
the walls. But the house is practical and man-sized, and still

proclaims the practicality and eccentric independence of the man. And it includes some lovely loot and some very judicious purchases, made when the Duke was Ambassador in Paris. It is basically a Victorian house. Inside it is a place to like rather than extravagantly to admire. Its opening to the public was the climax of these strange two days.

The Observer, 28 July 1974

The Times as it was

Journalists are a confraternity, every bit as separate as clerics, lawyers or doctors. Rightly and healthily we tend to be disliked – less than lawyers, more than clerics. Because we appear to have a fundamentally irresponsible power, because we are usually the bearers of bad news, because people tend overwhelmingly to buy the most vulgar of our products, the proper guilt of society is often loaded upon our scapegoat trade. In return, journalists have developed an attitude of *contra mundum*. We are more often lied to than we tell lies. We tend to delight in one another's company. We quarrel more eloquently than most men. Statistically, we are reported to be less alcoholic than the three professions I began with. But we have a fellow feeling, a loyalty to our trade that transcends circulation wars, the resentments caused by a failure in cheque-book journalism, and the fact that our reputations rise and fall like billows. If you wound one of us, we all bleed a little. And if you destroy one of our organs, we all feel the victims of grievous bodily harm. The possibility of the death of *The Times* is almost intolerable to almost all of us.

The Press can be nauseating about the freedom of the Press and the subject only becomes really convincing when talked about by non-pressmen. But *The Times* is something rare. It is not a mass circulation paper. Intellectual and moral excellence will not win any newspaper that. But, with the *Sunday Times* and its supplements, *The Times* was (and I hope will be again) part of the governance of the United Kingdom. People did not crowd to buy *The Times*, and yet its influence was vast and occasionally obvious. There were historical reasons for this. It was started in 1785 as the *Daily Universal Register*. It became *The Times* in 1788. Its proprietors were the successive generations of the Walter family. It introduced the idea that the Press had a proper, responsible and creative role to play in national affairs. Before that politicians regarded it, not as an institution working within the undefined frontiers of an unwritten constitution, but as a form of subversion, as an intolerable intrusion upon the gentleman's prerogative to govern, as a blunt and unfair weapon of opposition, as a thing that could only concern vulgarians. It established this right and duty to intrude once and for all during the Crimean War when it very bravely exposed the innate incompetence of our betters.

It has had its bad times before. Perhaps the worst was when it printed in good faith a letter by Parnell that a Commission found to be forged. That was in 1889. Its prestige and its finances suffered. But it survived. Though it made some fearful errors of pontifical judgement at times of crisis – notably in its attitude to Hitler in the 1930s – it never lost its august authority and all the time it changed, developing and adapting – for there is no true continuity within the history of any honest newspaper.

The present *Times* has developed a lighter and more elegant touch. It allows columnists to behave like prima donnas on their *chaise longues*. It has allowed a light, Senior Common Room sort of touch in its news columns. It has taken to cool reason. Among the Other Ranks, the hacks, the reporters, the scribblers, call them what you like, there is seldom animosity. The same curious comradeship appears in real battle. But we cannot afford to be diminished any further, nor can the public life of this country. Any government would be easier to replace than the whole set-up of the *Times* group.

Pray God, then they are only going into a temporary coma. We have in this country the best and almost the worst newspapers in the world. Each time one of them dies we are all the poorer because the variety is reduced and the day of no choice, of *Pravda* or *Osservatore Romano*, is brought a little closer. And even if that is not the actual day of tyranny, it is certainly the day of boredom. But it is more important even than that. If *The Times* goes down, we shall all indirectly and infinitely be the poorer in spirit. If self-interest on either side takes precedence over such an institution, we will be appallingly the more poor in public life.   *The Observer, 2 December 1978*

Publication of Times Newspapers Ltd was suspended from 1 December 1978 to 13 November 1979 because of a strike.

Trooping the Colour

The Queen's Colour of the Irish Guards was trooped before Her Majesty, mounted side-saddle, on Horse Guards Parade yesterday. The weather after a night of storm was dull as lead. Yet it was a slightly unusual Birthday Parade. This year is the eightieth anniversary of the founding of the Irish Guards, the fourth regiment of Foot Guards. It was formed by Queen Victoria in her great old age on 1 April 1900 to commemorate the gallantry of Irish regiments, of which there used to be many, during the South African War. This year is also the eightieth birthday of the Queen Mother who watched the parade from the window of Wellington's old office in what used to be the headquarters of the Army, in Kent's masterpiece of the Horse Guards. She has a special relationship with the regiment and has often distributed the shamrock on St. Patrick's Day on parade, this year in the pouring rain.

The Irish Guards, with only one battalion in peace-time, has developed a highly individual character. It cannot serve in Northern Ireland, since that might bring loyalties, dormant in England and other stations, dangerously close to the surface. As highly trained soldiers, retired Irish Guardsmen are in considerable demand by extremists on both sides of that dispute. That is inevitable. But the traditional parade passed yesterday without incident. The massed bands played what was perhaps a different class of music, like 'Believe me, if all these Endearing Young Charms', 'In Dublin's Fair City,' 'Slattery's Mounted Foot,' 'Mountains of Mourne' and 'Wild Colonial Boy', which is a song that glories in anarchic rebellion.

The Queen, suddenly transformed into a celebrant, went through her slow, hieratic moves, riding down the ranks, saluting her mother and saluting the Colour again and again, and each of the divisions of Guards as they marched tensely past her, the officers shouting orders, the markers on the stamping flanks shouting to the officers when it was safe to make the next move, the warrant officers at the rear, correcting the kinks in the line, the band wheeling like a great melodious mob which had found a purpose. Perhaps the great moment is when they 'troop' the Colour through the lines of the saluting soldiers. A 19-year-old officer carries the semi-sacred object and not even a Monstrance in Spain is greeted with more honour. The massive crown, topped with rich embroidery, towers over the troops while its escort moves through the ranks in a curiously balletic movement.

The Queen, behind the bands, led the lot back to Buckingham Palace. *The Observer, 15 June 1980*

He described the celebration in Westminster of the 1500th anniversary of the death of St. Benedict.

Celebrating St. Benedict in Cathedral and Abbey

Not since I was young have I seen such unabashed splendour in the Cathedral. (How maddening it must be for people in Birmingham and Liverpool to hear complacent Londoners talk thus about their mother church and expect every one else to understand.) Not being adept at mental prayer, I find these great public and ceremonial acts of prayer deeply satisfying. You are worshipping, I think, with your body and mind and heart and that fastidious side that delights in beauty and all sustained, as in a war, by the loyalty and temporary love of those around you, by the presence of a company of fellow Christians.

The monks poured in as if a black and white tap had been turned on. Unlike British regiments, they are not readily, even by me, recognisable in their habits. All were of the Benedictine family. Some were Cistercians. Some Black Monks wear white. You cannot tell an Anglican from a Catholic monk by the cut of his jib. In front of nearly 500 monks and nuns, the

Cathedral pulled its stops out. True I do not get to this church on great feasts, but I have the impression that the traditional splendours are out of fashion and the Cardinal mostly presides like a priest from a chair behind an altar set uneasily in the centre of the sanctuary. This time, while all the marble and mosaic and metal work were ablaze with light, the vast high altar under its triumphal arch of largely yellow marble, was left in crepuscular dismissal. Not even the candles on this altar were lit.

But the Cardinal was back upon the throne, which must be at once the most splendid and the least comfortable chair in the kingdom. (It is in fact a near copy by the cathedral architect of the Pope's episcopal chair in his cathedral of St. John Lateran.) They put splendid great cushions on it in the liturgical colours which must ease it a bit. He went up into the pulpit, which is like a royal box upon stilts. He went with candles and crozier and mitre bearers so that he spoke out of a little, devout court of fellow Catholics. He sat on his throne with abbots on each side of him and one apart on his left, just as they did when I was a child, and they had deacons of the throne and an assistant priest. It went on for at least two hours and it was good.

As soon as the Mass was over, it was up, up, up and away down the length of Queen Victoria Street to the Abbey. I hared off for a bus. The monks and nuns got a cup of tea in the Cathedral hall and arrived by coach loads. I was beginning to feel rather old.

The Abbey is an astonishing place. It seldom gets the credit for being the superb piece of rather French Gothic that most of it is. It is fashionable to decry the forests of funeral sculpture and the walls scaled with monuments, (including one to that Major André whom the Americans executed as a spy; General Washington wept as he signed the death warrant). But look at them as eccentric works of art and they become a secular delight to add to the sacred. It is the most fascinating place in London to walk round, but, alas, this has become almost impossible. It is now loud with tourists who queue to get in, wearing their cameras like pilgrims' badges.

I sat in the nave and faced the gloriously gilded screen that is wide enough to hold a choir and orchestra for Coronations. The organ fair blasted away and the place quickly filled. Then the procession again. Monks and nuns filled the choir stalls which had been built for them. The Primate and the Cardinal walked in. The Dean and his chapter and the deans of those cathedrals that once had Benedictine priors and a lady in bright lipstick carrying a mace and a server with a strange ivory processional cross all disappeared behind the screen. All sumptuously apparelled. Unlike the monks. This disappearance was just right. The monks used to worship in private. And the murmur of their song and the flicker of their candles and the perishing cold of their stone floors and a visit to the shrines was what the people got. Abbey churches were not public places, but highly professional ones.

This time the Abbey had not set out their great sideboard display of golden vessels on the high altar as they do on major Anglican occasions. But all the tapers everywhere were lit. It should be remembered that on the first occasion Elizabeth Tudor visited the Abbey, the Community that had been restored by Mary met her ceremonially at the door with candles in their hands. She told them to put out their tapers since she could see perfectly well. That was the sentence of monastic extinction. And then they sang Vespers. It was not Solesmes standard, it was very English, which means it is less etiolated and more open air. It was also sung by a number that would have shamed even the old Yorkshire choral societies who used to blast out the Messiah as if they were repelling boarders. And the singers came from so many different houses, congregations and orders that it was surprising that there was not the equivalent of a choral punch-up. But it was riveting and one forgot one's exhaustion and hunger and anxiety about a train home. And the other thing. The Dean preached superbly but had not been well briefed on the subtleties of the precedence in the English Benedictine Congregation. There'll be bitterness in some cloisters for months to come. Not bitterness really, but there will be comments. No matter. The Abbey did them superbly in their own house.

There was a lady in the Abbey who joined in accurately in all the plainsong, even the twiddly bits. She bowed like any monk and was clearly some monastic groupie. Maddening! And quite wrong. But we were not at the opera and it might have been thought discourteous if I had hissed 'Shut up!' But I was sorely tempted. (In the Cathedral there had been another lady who went on trilling her notes long after everyone else had stopped. But there I did not dare to turn to identify her.) How do you greet old friends in solemn procession? 'Custody of the eyes' is one of the monastic virtues in choir. Well you can't stare about you too much when there is another bank of monks or nuns dead opposite, can you? Unexpectedly I was greeted by an old friend in the procession. He was discreet. I gave a sort of silent football cheer. Some monks walked out of the Abbey as recollected as can be. Others smiled and made little gestures with their hands which meant 'See you for a pint in the Bunch of Grapes afterwards'. I cut some acquaintances and friends dead and feel bad about it. But everyone was turned towards the aisle in the end and it became a sort of mobile reception. And so it should be after a Te Deum sung by the only people left alive who know the tune. Some of the nuns were having a ball, greeting friends, touching shoulders, beaming with the sort of joy that sometimes comes from alcohol. Honesty compels me to admit that their singing was better than that of the monks.

At vespers they sang a hymn to St. Benedict. I had long forgotten the tune which is that of *Iste Confessor*. It starts *Gemma caelestis pretiosa Regis*. It is translated, first verse:

'Pattern of monks, and precious gem
Of Christ's eternal diadem,
Keep us, on this our worldly way,
Unspotted from the world's decay.'

There's an 18th century cream cake of a piece of poesy for you. Dryden? He translated a great deal for the Catholics. Both he and Pope (the other poet) were meant to be Catholics. No, I think it was translated by the classics master at Ampleforth who got bored of trying to teach me Latin, the remarkable Walter Shewring. A literary distraction. A pleasurable distraction in the jollity of the tune. How much better than any of the new pop tunes, but not really suitable for parish use. Final distractions. Exhaustion. Death of my feet. No buses. No taxis. A protestant sort of drizzle. If I'm too old for this sort of thing I'm too old for anything. But oh! I do wish great Churches had small loos.

The Catholic Herald, 18 July 1980

Gardens were always a popular theme, whether it was allotments, or his own, or his parish's. The first of these next four pieces appeared on the front page of The Observer *on the Sunday before a General Election when politics were taboo.*

Snails

Snails more than Tories now concern us. It may not be a national concern but in Hampshire, if you have a garden, they present a problem not like income tax but more puzzling than Mrs. Thatcher. It is unthinkable that they be stamped upon, though that would probably be the kindest thing you could do. They have survived the black winter and are now hard at work on the most delicate of our leaves. That plants that have survived the burning of the winter cold should now be eaten is curiously unfair.

There are no ground rules about snails. The upper classes may be blamed for their attitude to foxes. The lower classes are free to do what they do with fishes caught in the rain from old gravel pits. There is no justice. No one pities snails. Traditionally they should be popped in buckets of salt water which must provide a fearful death. Or you can buy chemical pellets that make them fizz to death and which must wreak the ultimate type of cruelty in defence of lettuces. Or, most convenient, they can be thrown over the garden wall into the paradise next door. This causes no suffering but the idea of one's neighbour being confronted with a flying snail is daunting and it would be reported and to be known as a snail tosser would mean social death. I have, however, discovered the perfect, the cowardly solution. You find your snail – and there never seem to be any small snails – and you pick it up gently and put it in the most exposed place you can find. With any luck a thrush will be watching and will kill and eat it in a very terrible way. This method could be described as a recycling and it is therefore ecologically acceptable. It is more widely used in Britain than is generally accepted. And it gives the snail, like the fox and the coarse fish, at least a sporting chance.

If coarse fishing is the chief participatory popular sport in England, the creation and care of gardens is the island's chief art form. The best book that any Sitwell ever wrote was by Sir

George – the eccentric and rather nasty father, damned so successfully by Sir Osbert. It was about gardens. He laid down a rule, as surely as any Pope, that gardens should be silvery grey. A touch of pale blue here and there was just permissible. His was not a cottage garden, but a place of terraces and statuary, lending dignity to a great house set in an industrial landscape. Anyone who followed his advice – like me – is desolate. All those silver grey plants have died, as if seared by heat. But there is no neat pattern. Yellow butterflies were out at Easter. Creeping Jenny – a dreary ground cover – has enjoyed itself. Giant hogweed, that grows so quick and so tall that it seems to walk towards the house in the night, has had a ball. Really vicious weeds like ground elder which, like heretics, must be burned rather than put on the compost heap, have carpeted the corners of the gardens of the middle classes. Lawns have become moss patches. Other things have gone wrong too. House martins, swifts, and swallows were always due here on 17 April. None has yet arrived and the mud house one sort of them built under the eave is still empty. The blossom on barren cherry trees has never been brighter and the daffodils, which are the most boring flowers in the world, have done splendidly. But then so have the snails – and their unmentionable sisters, the slugs. Reverence For Life goes towards its own frontier. Toads are admitted. Snails are out.

The Observer, 29 April 1979

Mauve fingers

Some of the most revolting verses and some of the most repellent songs have been written about the English garden. There is one verse that includes the line: 'A garden is a lovesome thing, God wot', and another:

'One is nearer to God's Heart in a garden
Than anywhere else on earth.'

Both statements are utterly indefensible. The English garden is a battlefield, a stricken field, a disaster area.

The English are compulsive gardeners. Far into old age they heave and strain at forking over and breaking great lumps of mud on dismal patches of earth called 'allotments' in the shadow of blackened factories and satanic mills. They cram the gardens in front of, and behind their suburban houses with flowers that really do look like the illustrations on seed packets. Municipalities go to great expense to reproduce curiously shaped beds of flowers in unsuitable places that look either like plates of vegetables or squashed hats. All this is supposed to be the admiration of the world. The admiration is uncritical. It tolerates the tousled roses in half-a-dozen shades of pink, the petunias screaming at each other in mauve and scarlet, the hateful zinnia and the horrid marigold. The strange thing is that they are grown at all with such love and effort.

However, I have a garden. An elderly German noblewoman visited it the other day and exclaimed when she saw it: 'Ah, un veritable jardin de curé.' Germans it seems break into French when they are deeply moved. What, apparently, she meant was that it was a typical English garden, a mess without design, bursting with uncontrollable ripeness. I love it dearly. I am hooked. All my petunias are purple. Good gardeners in England are said to have green fingers. Mine are mauve. If I come to it late at night from London, I go around it with a torch to see if another new flower has lifted its episcopally-coloured head during the week. The garden is in Hampshire. For a generation it had been a steady source of food for the farm workers who lived in the solid little house which is now the envy of intellectuals. The lawns are rough and studded with flints. The hedge would keep out lions. This half-acre is at once the playground and the cafeteria of hares, pheasants, partridge, sparrows, moles, shrew, mice and pigeons. Vast and frightening, pale grey owls moan over it. It is lost, an oasis of desolation in the middle of a beautifully-tended estate farm.

When I came to it, I had read a curious book on gardening by Sir George Sitwell who, the father of Osbert, Edith and Sacheverell Sitwell, had endured life in a vast Italian villa of the best period. He believed that flowers were vulgar, and that the colours of gardens should be silver and grey. But the temptations are too strong. A visit to the shop in Alresford, and in go the bootleg seeds and up come the heretical plants – red, yellow and, of course, mauve. In one corner thirty shillings worth of assorted shrubs bought from a newspaper advertisement has turned into a Victorian thicket of dark green leaves, and is now impenetrable. There is a long vegetable patch. Perhaps there is some lack of skill here. Lettuces go to seed before they are ready for picking. Cabbages grow like splendid heraldic flowers and never have a heart. Potatoes produce dozens of delicious little buttons. We grow the smallest peas and the most contorted beans in Europe. A whole row of beetroot just disappears during an absence of five days. Carrots come up like the fangs of a small carnivorous animal. Marrows rot on the vine.

I planted a cherry tree four years ago. In all that time it has produced one cherry which, despite the anti-bird defence set up around it, fell off before it was ripe. This pampered tree this year was covered with a biblical plague of small, black, disgusting insects which crinkled the leaves and stopped any fruit at all. Only the root artichokes flourish, an unpleasant vegetable which is suitable only for a windy soup. They have taken over their own corner and cannot be driven back.

Then there is the expense. The shed is full of rotary and conventional lawn mowers, the shelf of chemicals, the festering sack of dried blood, the stinking fertilizers that bring me out in spots, insecticides that make children sick. But this year my gladioli, shoved in without care among the potatoes, dozens of them, came up large, flamboyant, un-English and of course, largely mauvish. They won first prize in the village flower show. They are Jamaican in their exuberance and the village did not wholly approve. But perhaps it is a consolation from that English god of gardens to which I am now a slave.

The Observer, Autumn 1967

O'Donovan's Fourth Law

Other parishes in Britain may have their troubles. Some may have a crippling debt. Some may have a pastor with an early counter-Reformation cast of mind. We have weeds. In fact, our church is set upon a high bank with a great lawn all around. You could build a marvellous set of Spanish Steps up the bank to culminate in the wooden and excellent austerity of the church itself. Baroque saints could point the way upwards in a whirlwind of pious drapery. But they would be irresistible to the creative impulses of the local schoolchildren. And, anyway we cannot afford them. And they would seem un-English in so English a place. And someone would fall down them and sue. So we have this high, steep, grassy bank. Except that no blade of grass has a chance on it. It is, or was, covered with a rich variety of weeds. It even acquired a sort of fascinating and primeval horror.

In the Gospel there was a deal of distress about darnel in the wheat sowed by some saboteur. I suspect we had darnel among our thistles and docks. We could not afford a real gardener, and even the most horticultural ladies quailed before our spiky jungle. It was becoming a bit of a scandal. Protestants were beginning to raise their eyebrows. Then someone had an idea. The parish threw a barbecue party preceded by an hour's work among the weeds. It was an enchanting Saturday evening. About forty people turned up bearing forks (called "prongs" here), thick gloves, buckets and sickles. It became genuinely joyous. And when the hour was over, we moved to the *Jardin du Curé*, which is a small sunken lawn hidden behind the small house attached to the church. Here there were buns and sausages and onions and sauce and a plenitude of wine and cider (and, for all I know, Coca-Cola) and we were really a community.

I fear this achievement is rare anywhere. *It is no good asking for volunteers* – O'Donovan's Fourth Law – but with gentle leadership and initiative, it really works. Personally I cleared about three square feet of flower bed of every sort of darnel and evil root. So there is one small perfect patch. The rest of the grounds looks as if it had been given a sort of old army short-back-and-sides haircut. And the weeds will grow again. Which will be a marvellous excuse for doing the whole thing again next year.   *The Catholic Herald, 13 October 1978*

Allotments

Another one of those large and meticulous and majestic and drily donnish reports of which the British are the world's masters has been issued by Her Majesty's Stationery Office.★ This one, costing two guineas, concerns the past, present and future of allotments. These are those horticultural slums on the outskirts of industrial towns and the bald and scabrous patches in the middle of villages. You pass them in trains slowing down for the station and regard their undoubted ugliness with a vague, self-satisfied benevolence. Because they are worthy places, dedicated to individual freedom, the British form of chaos, to eccentricity, to physical exercise and to the creative delight of growing something where there was nothing before and cutting down the household bills. For these are private places visited only by their tenants and by vandals who won't say no to a free cabbage or a bunch of dahlias for nothing.

These, as much as any leathery, port-scented club, are male preserves. Only 3.2 per cent of all allotment holders are women. There are half a million tenanted plots in England and Wales. These are places where a man can put up a shed and sit in his private gazebo behind a barrier of beans and read the paper and smoke and be away from home without self-reproach and contemplate the most satisfying of all possessions, which is land. Particularly in industrial towns, they are islands of a self-expression at least as authentic as that permitted to a Sunday journalist. These are the plots that spawn the ferocious vegetable shows where onions, like severed heads, are laid out on dishes and marrows shown as fat, smooth and useless as Byzantine eunuchs. These produce the great, sleek leeks and the rattling peas. These are the places where retired people (22 per cent of all allotment holders) feel still useful and busy. They exist abroad but there they are less anarchic, more controlled. Outside Warsaw, for example, they have become the extension of inadequate flats, exploding with flowers and fruit and containing miniature houses. In Denmark they are ordered and practical and intended to make money. In Germany they are planned like parks. But in Britain you very nearly do as you please – except that in a few of them you may not work there on Sunday and in many of them you may not keep livestock, except bees. But alas, they are declining. Local authorities do not obey their statutory obligations to provide them. Planners resent the loss of land, in some areas worth £15,000 to £20,000 an acre, and they dislike the scrubby and desolate air of most such places.

Allotments started in a recognisable way as a guilt-ridden

reaction to the condition of those people who could not be blamed for their plight. During the Enclosures, some wealthy landlords provided consolidated plots for their cottagers. And by the General Enclosure Act of 1845, the Enclosure Commissioners were enjoined to provide plots for the 'labouring poor.' Among the arguments in their favour was that these plots would induce 'grateful respect' for those who provided them. Of course there was opposition. Prosperous farmers in need of labour thought them a sinful waste of man-hours. Philanthropists objected that they were a substitute for decent wages, a sort of grow-your-own poor rate. But they were too obviously worthy to be stopped. There was a spectacular spread of them in the First World War. In the Second World War, 10 per cent of Britain's food came from allotments and private gardens. These derelict and rather tatty looking places have a noble record.

[Departmental Committee of Inquiry into Allotments, a report published by HMSO. £2.2s]   *The Observer, 9 November 1969*

Thoughts on Pope John

'I am glad to hear the good news about the repairs at home, but I am sorry that the lavatory has not yet been put in order. You must know that it is by the state of the lavatory that a family is judged.' This was written with real and ancient wisdom to the sisters, Ancilla and Maria, in June, 1926, by that sensible but simple man who became Pope John XXIII. And if anyone thinks it is bad taste to quote such a thing, he is not on my side, no friend, a dark-souled man and quite destitute of the blinding splendour of humility.

I remember once being in Budapest and talking to some students. For a moment the world looked sweet and promising. There was Kennedy in the White House who seemed to be the most exciting elected person since Lincoln. There was also Khrushchev in the Kremlin. He used to get tipsy in public which, at least for a politician, is better than doing it in private. He had left in him, despite his appalling personal history, some appreciation of the concept of love. When it was safe to do so, he was shocked by the record of Stalin. There was Pope John, and the Hungarian students – who evaporated like a thin puddle of water when they thought that the police were listening to our talk – put him ahead of both the others, not for his power, but for his goodness. Our talk was in a coffee shop. My photographer was on the other side of the narrow street taking pictures of po-faced ladies having their hair done in a way that Lenin surely never envisaged. But then, but then, for a few months rationality and charity seemed practically possible. And Pope John was the centre and the architect of this international tolerance and love.

When he died some ludicrous person suggested that I might write his life. I read his writings and, God forgive me, I thought them threadbare. Now, in a sudden awareness of age and the quiet and unforgiving approach of Death, I begin to understand a man who makes a glorious, kitchen-sink sense of our Faith. From Sophia in 1930, he wrote: 'Here too, as everywhere, it is the unbridled tongue that ruins everything.' Collapse of stout Charterhouse. I saw him once in the Sistine Chapel. He was hurried in by grandly unsuitable guards. He looked old and ill and white-faced and pudding fat and one's heart went out in a barren and ludicrous desire to help. He wore a tight fur-edged hood over his head. I cannot remember why, but the occasion was meant to be for journalists. As always in Rome, the occasion got out of control. Not only princes of the most doubtful lineage but people who were merely rich were crammed into the places reserved for the undemanding us. He stepped off the dais, set up under the most daring work of art that man has ever tried, and moved, like the Queen on a 'walk-about', to talk with the journalists. He spoke to only two before the noble guard moved him on. One of them was from *Izvestia* and the other from *Pravda*. And one of them wept.

The thing about him was that he was almost as sensible as to be an Englishman. He wrote about an aunt who had not reproduced: 'The Lord denied her the grace of motherhood so that she might more easily give all her loving care and attentive service to the family of her brothers and sisters.' What a wise old gentleman! He said: 'So let us continue from day to day in holiness and cheerfulness.' It's the last noun I like best, and I never, alas, took wine with him.   *The Catholic Herald, 2 June 1978*

On understanding

A kindly convert, in a letter, took me to task for not under-standing 'the working class' – a fearful accusation that might easily lead to my ending, hung from a lamp post. No, I do not understand the working class, nor do I understand Pro-tonotaries Apostolic, or Regius Professors of History at Oxford, or politicians who chose to run for office because they like office more than goodness, or people who despise jour-nalists, or priests who quit the Church to get married, or Ul-ster Protestants of the more weird sort, or Archbishop Lefebvre, and least of all Fr. Morgan of that poor good man's persuasion. Nor do I understand myself. No man has a right to claim really to understand anything, except perhaps love or an account sheet.

I write this because, lately and long, I have seen priests in hospital helping the sick. Some sad Catholic patients fear the priests, lest they come as a presage of death. It looks the most deadly dull work there is. But of course it is the best thing a priest can do – better even than giving alms to the poor. This is their job. I was put in my place by one recently, when I suggested the job might be routine. One thinks of a politician with a live vote to gain: but the good priest thinks of a soul to help or a frightened person to save or a drugged creature to dig-nify. I have been most kindly treated in the past by the noblest of priests in hospital. I do not understand the working classes; it looks as if I do not understand the nature, the essential sacra-mental nature, of the priesthood. But then, only a very coarse man would ever say that he understood anything completely.

The Catholic Herald, 12 August 1977

Collared clergy

The Bishop of Chester (C of E) has put his foot down. He wants to make it mandatory for his clergy to wear clerical col-lars when on duty. This raises the question of when a priest is not on duty. The second question is who is going to take a blind bit of notice. I intend no discourtesy but the Middle Way, the *via media*, of the Anglican Church is almost as wide as it is long and most Anglicans, I would hazard, are proud of this and compare their state as glorious and English in comparison with the imagined rigidity of Rome. An Anglican clergyman has to do something pretty scandalous to be booted out of his living or it must be proved that pastoral communications have broken down within the parish. I don't think that anyone in Chester is going to be driven into the Mountains of Moab for wearing the wrong collar.

Take another look at the 'dog collar'. It really is a ludicrous item of clothing. It looks uncomfortable. It looks as if its wearer were being humiliated with some peculiar badge. Clerical every day walking out uniform is comparatively new. St. Benedict just advised some suitable local cloth. But the orders did later put on great, enveloping uniforms, if only to save them from liturgical hypothermia in ancient choirs. I do not know what the poor parish priest before the Reformation wore about his daily life. Once all educated priests wore cassocks except when out hunting or in bed. In France, for example, they wore bands that flapped from the neck. All the pictures of the Curé d'Ars show the bands of the sort that our barristers still wear in court and which are sported by the dignitaries of Oxford and Cambridge on their more delicious occasions.

The clerical collar, as far as I can discover, came to Britain, wafted by Pius IX and insisted upon by Archbishop Manning. In England when the Catholic priests emerged from their imposed secrecy, they wore black suits and linen stocks that came up to their ears. Even monks stumped into their cut price choirs dressed like farmers in mourning.

What should the well dressed priest wear? A friend – a fierce and most dangerous cleric – says he invented that little slip of celluloid that slips into a sort of pocket at the neck and can be whipped out if the party is getting out of control. It is in fact oddly elegant. Ronnie Knox used to wear a Roman job as big as a horse-collar. It was a very narrow thing. Fr. D'Arcy wore a towering Roman job that looked like the Castel San Angelo wound about his neck. I never saw him in anything else. Cardinal Heenan was a high collar man, but I've seen him whip it off – and in Rome – and say, 'phew!' Most young priests hate the things – unless they accept them as part of their calvary. Personally – old biretta hat that I am – they can wear what they like. I do, however, think that there should be some public sign about their person that they and God have set themselves aside a little. But, the bliss of it, it is not a very important question. I think that ordinary people take some comfort in the outward sign of some man's inner commitment. I'm told, mind you I'm only told, that it's possible in Portugal for a young priest never even to have owned such a thing.

The Catholic Herald, 17 October 1980

Blood sports and morality

You are not meant either to envy or resent the status and living conditions of the Royals. And when they are attacked for 'giving a bad example' by going fox hunting, I feel an indignation and compassion for them which is probably quite uncalled for. What fun it would be to own all those enormous houses, with lots of small ones too if you wanted to live the simple life on beer and sausages for a bit. What fun not even to know what you own, with enough gorgeous bric-a-brac to keep a museum gallery for ever full (the Queen's Gallery in London) with ever changing exhibitions.

Their ancestors were pretty good collectors. Charles I was a superb buyer but Cromwell flogged most of his pictures to the Tsars and founded the basis of the Hermitage collection in St. Petersburg. George III was good on clocks. The Prince Regent got a thing or two out of the debris of the French Revolution. The Prince Consort practically introduced the Italian Primitives to the country. Queen Victoria used to buy a suitable contemporary picture every year but did not believe it right to pay more than something like £70. She always got her picture. How pleasant to find a Canaletto used as a splash board in a servant's bedroom in a Palace. And you don't have to bother about your etchings, you have those portfolios of Leonardo drawings in the library.

Mind you there are drawbacks as there are in every job – the work. All those tours – alleviated by superb staff work. And where do all the presents go? On the many royal tours I have attended as a journalist, I have seen them loaded down with war canoes, cloaks made of feathers, books of commemorative photographs, and a herd of various animal toys for the children. They can't all go to the Great Ormond Street Hospital for Children. Of course, there are other drawbacks. The speeches, the occasional insolent student, the marvellous, deadly food. For, wherever you go, some cook has done her/his best and is peering from the kitchen to see how much of the saddle of lamb you are eating. And then every week, if you are the Monarch and not a fringe Royal, the Prime Minister calls to keep you in the picture. Of course you get red boxes of reports to read. But there is nothing anyway you can do about it. Even some of Queen Victoria's most frantic royal advice got ignored.

But then Royals are fair game for three sorts of criticism. There is the straight, pseudo-republican, you-cost-too-much sort. There is a sort of innocence here. There is a popular press approach in which, under the guise of giving loyal advice, some paper is able to criticise and to insinuate. Much better the direct insults of *Private Eye* or Wee Willie Hamilton, MP. But I detest the tactics of the anti-fox hunters who would make them the scapegoats for this whole not particularly blood-thirsty nation and insist they stop bouncing about the country in elegant clothes seeking the ritual death of a fox. I'm not a bit surprised if occasionally, after they have wielded air sprays at the hounds, some splendid woman past her prime on a horse lashes out a bit or the retired colonel who is people's warden in his parish church rides his horse at some protestor.

Now Catholic newspapers, and for all that I know every other sort of newspaper, are subject to a great deal of animal propaganda. Some of it is horrid. Some of it is brave and passionate. Some of it seems informed by hate and envy rather than by love. The first Bishop of Arundel and Brighton, the late David Cashman, was a lovely man. He once said that one of the great pleasures of his life was shooting. This statement was picked up by the *Daily Mirror*, and was splashed across the front page. To his vast honour he never claimed that some reporter – usually as fair game as any stoat – had misquoted him, even though for a day or two he was libelled as a blood-thirsty bishop. I have too many friends who shoot and hunt and worship God with a humble and sophisticated piety above mine to blame people who enjoy these pleasures. Because I have not been tempted by this sport, nor indeed have had much chance to practise it, this is the least of all arguments why I should take up arms against it.

The attitude of the Church has been unworried about the whole matter. Animals were created for the use of humans though it is true that they were not made for their pleasure. Yet high ecclesiastics have often indulged in the chase. One post-Reformation Archbishop of Canterbury killed a keeper while out stag hunting and, poor fellow, was suspended from his priestly functions for shedding human blood. Huntsmen even have their own patron saint. This is St. Hubert who flourished in the seventh century. He is said to have been the son of the Duke of Aquitaine and a leader of royal courts, charming and utterly committed to the chase. He was out hunting when most good people were in church one Good Friday. He was chasing a magnificent stag when the animal stopped and turned and looked at him and he saw that it had a crucifix between its antlers. He then heard a voice telling him that he would go down into hell unless he began to lead a holy life. He went at once to Maastricht, one of those rich little Low Country cities whose fate is for ever to be fought over. His wife died. He gave his son to his brother and his money to the poor. He resigned his titles and became the first Bishop of Liège. To generations of Catholics his story has not discouraged, it has positively sanctified the hunt. His feast used to fall on November 3. This day is now given to the Peruvian St. Martin de Porres who was of mixed blood and very kind to mice.

The formality, the dignity and the danger seem to me to confer a rightness on fox hunting. It is not a subject I could or would debate in public. I have not enough indignation left over from other things to condemn it and I confess I do not like the people who make such an ugly song and dance about it. And I am fascinated into silence by people who talk about horses. It is to break all the rules of our unwritten constitution to pick on the Royals for this particular sort of condemnation. This is a highly selective and suspect sort of indignation. Why is it never extended to coarse fishing. But that is a working class sport, cruel but sacrosanct.

We have got rid of cock-fighting – I saw it once in Bali and it was thrilling and horrifying and I left for the same reason that I left *Oh! Calcutta* at half time.

We have stopped otter hunting. Unlike Italians we do not shoot starlings, though I have eaten them in the oldest restaurant in the world (which is in Tokyo) and they are delicious. We do not set terriers on rats any more. We don't send children down the mines. But there is a Welsh boxer lying in a coma while I am writing this. I do not see how we can justify the continuation of this 'noble art'.

I have a faint suspicion that I have been inconclusive. But I thank God that the Church is not too conclusive about animals. And I hate the bullying tactics of those who would stop other people smoking or Prince Charles going out hunting.

The Catholic Herald, 3 October 1980

The story of a minority

It is a curious experience to be a Roman Catholic in England today. It is not disagreeable. It is attended by a few minor disadvantages. In politics your prospects are limited. In journalism your objectivity is, on certain subjects, suspect. Certain delicious jobs in education are naturally closed to you. And if you are a writer you are filed under a special, eccentric, and rather disliked category by most of the critics in the country. And then too – not to make too fine a point of it – we are still under minor and ancient disabilities. If a man were of the blood royal and if he then chose to embrace and endure the discipline of Rome, he could never be sovereign or stand in the succession. And for similar sound historical reasons that could not be justified in cold debate he could not be Lord Chancellor. In addition, though a Jew has been Prime Minister of Britain, or at least a racial Jew, and though the religiously touchy Americans have accepted a Catholic President, no Catholic could be Prime Minister of Britain. It is not against any law; it is merely unthinkable. And we do not resent these things: they are almost a part of our tradition too; and they are no great matter.

All these things are endurable and a Catholic cannot really blame the majority for enforcing them. To be a Catholic in England is to belong to a minority that does not know its place. Of course England is a body politic composed of minorities, particularly if you regard it in the light of religion. Even the Church by law established is a minority. And indeed the whole practising Christian body together is a minority. But the Catholic minority here is specially set apart by history and inclination. It is even set apart from its fellow minorities and majorities overseas. The Irish in Ireland regard it with considerable suspicion, if not dislike. The Americans find it incomparably grand, though with a tendency to superiority. The French appear to regard it as a sect for pious gentlefolk or even a diluted Protestantism, and it is fairly hard to convince the Italians that it exists. In fact it is an intensely English body. It shies away from excesses of ritual, from eccentric devotion, and it is more than a little suspicious of its own most glittering intellectuals. It is conservative – though perhaps even a majority of it votes Labour. It is conservative in practice and thought and of course in architecture, where we have never got over the fact that Pugin was one of our converts. It is intensely loyal to the Papacy and yet manages to maintain its strong, even stiff, national character. It also tends to be strongly monarchical and, of course, it is of its nature opposed to violent or revolutionary change. It is very definitely a proselytizing body, but then so are most Christian bodies. It prays regularly for the conversion of England, though joining it may prove a tedious, even daunting process. It is not always as generous as it should be to converts. There is less sense of parochial fellowship than in the Protestant churches. A man could worship for years at the same Sunday Mass, in the same pew, in the same large parish church, and never get to know one of his fellow-Catholics.

But in being a Catholic in England there is an overwhelming sense of belonging to a great and ancient and noble body. It is almost a sense of privilege. It brings many inconveniences in the form of duties that have to be done; but the fact remains that there is a worldly delight in being a Catholic in England that cancels out all the rest. I suspect that several other Christian communities in England could sincerely say precisely the same. I am not trying to be theological or even argumentative. Of the spiritual benefits of being a Catholic, of the colossal claims of the Church and of its consolations, I shall say nothing. I want only to talk of this now familiar body that is sunk into English life as surely and as naturally as the roots of a tree plunged into the ground. If we are separate and believe things which many consider outrageous or preposterous or rather sad, and if we owe an extra spiritual allegiance to a foreign ecclesiastical sovereign, we yet manage to integrate ourselves. We are, if you like, a limb of England rather than a malignant growth within its body. And this is due not so much to any wisdom or restraint on our part but to the tolerance of England. They have got used to our spires among theirs, to our unmistakable clergymen in the streets, to our nuns in their odd habits, to our occasional protests in the press, to our pundits laying down our law on television and radio. We are a facet of England as well as part of a universal Church. There are no Catholic political leaders, though there are Catholic politicians. There is, thank God, no Catholic vote. We manage or are allowed to belong. It is a remarkable achievement on somebody's part.

For the essential fact about Catholicism in England is that it is based on a historical grievance. The Catholic Church in England claims an unbroken succession, through Augustine and others, back to Apostolic times. Others make the same claim. But for us there obtrudes the fact of the Reformation, not as a triumph of reform or of English compromise or of spiritual rebirth, but as an overwhelming tragedy, as a disaster that all but broke the thread of sacred continuity. What to the majority of England seems a triumph of reason, to us – and to understate it – seems a terrible error. It also at times seems a sort of robbery. It is basic in our various attitudes of mind. If we go to visit a ruined monastery in a Yorkshire valley, to a Catholic it is not simply a charming example of the romantic landscape or a good example of an early English choir or an interesting variation of the Cistercian lay-out. It is a place from which the monks were driven out; it is a place whose vestments and sacred vessels were seized and sold or destroyed; it is a place from which the sacrament was rudely banished. A great cathedral, exquisitely preserved and improved in the Anglican manner, is both a source of national pride and of personal sorrow. It is easy for us to admire, even to love, the sonority and dignity of the Anglican ritual, to admire the decency and devotion of their priests. It is easy, too, to accept the fact that if the cathedrals were ours they would be littered now with objects of devotion so meretricious, so debased and degenerate in form, that half the visual delight would be gone. But the sadness, the longing, the cupidity remains. The old chant, the ancient ritual, the true presence are gone, and to us, at least, it seems that the buildings are being used for purposes other than their builders intended. We feel that our ancestors and ourselves have been deprived of their rights.

We start with a somewhat different view of English history. I say we start, because time and experience of other views blunt the sharpness of our interpretation. But for us Henry VIII, Elizabeth I, and Cromwell are not the great lusty heroes of England, but the people who tried to destroy the old faith. And our heroes are martyrs like More and Fisher and Campion. We know exactly how they died and we think we know why they died: and these we cherish, as heroes as much as saints, men who were great by any standards; and with them a huge company of more ordinary men and women, and all so immediate, so explicable, so open and so English that it seems almost odd to expect miracles and wonders of them in the Italian manner. But if we are not divided among ourselves, there are several sorts of English Catholics. There are first what used to be called the old Catholics. These are essentially the descendants of the county families who literally kept the faith during the long, boring years of persecution. They paid their recusancy fines; they sent sons and cousins to be educated in exiled English seminaries in France, Spain, and Portugal. Some became priests, some harboured priests and paid for it. They intermarried and some of them grew rich of it. They played almost no part in the life of England. They survived. To these must be added the many converts of the second spring in the nineteenth century. Originally they opposed the old Catholics as too conservative and too far from the continental excitements of the Church. Today the descendants of all these remain a lay power within the Church. They are not churchy people; they have no passion for ritual or the fine points of dogma; they tend to treat priests as a professional class whose proper place is at the altar and they only adopt and embrace a special few of them. They are quietly, utterly loyal to the faith of their fathers, to the dull heroism of their own history. They are pious, unostentatious, but again, above all, loyal – as if it were unthinkable to be anything else but a Mass-goer. To them, to be a Catholic in England is the most natural thing in the world, not worth arguing about, ill-mannered to proclaim. In a very different way, their Catholicism is as natural as that of a Spanish peasant and yet it is as English as anything in England. Its attendant sin is snobbery; its glory is faithfulness, simplicity, and uncomplicated goodness. Much larger is the group of Irish Catholics. They came here with a load of historical sorrow that was heavier even than that of the Poles. Most of them have shed it and many of them shed their faith too in the process. But they remain the flesh that clothes and animates the Church in England. Having no leaders of their own, they took the priests. The bishops are their aristocracy. They do not seek for any great beauty in their services, only for familiar prayers and devotions, the essential Mass and of course the Sacraments – particularly at the point of death. The young men prefer to stand at the back of the church during the mysteries. The women cling to their rosaries. They are the despair of liturgical reformers. The Church in England would be a sad and etiolated little sect without them, yet they have not made it an Irish overseas church. England has, gently this time, reasserted itself and a decent compromise has been made.

There are dozens of other sorts. There are professional Catholics. There are Catholics who were nothing much, but who happened to marry Catholics and so took it up for the sake of the children or peace in the home. There are converts seeking authority, and converts who reached it all via the intellect and still sadden for the splendours and decorum of the Anglican Church. There are Catholics who would knock you down at a rude word about the Virgin Mother and yet have not been to church for years. There are Catholics who believe the priests are on the make, but cannot keep away from it. There are Catholics who dare not give it up, just in case it is true. And there are saints and good sinners and there are those who have never thought and never will think of anything else. Things are changing now – and wholly for the better. The sense of grievance is lifting; so is the hostility and suspicion. In tolerance and courtesy, the Catholics have not yet gone as far as the Anglicans. But from out of that implacable, overwhelming confidence, from out of that certainty of the absolute truth that properly sets Catholics apart, there is swiftly emerging the idea that if the others are wrong, at least it is not their fault.

This is an unprecedented tolerance. At last we are beginning to appreciate the virtues of our separated brethren. That may sound intolerably smug – and of course we are – but it is one of the sweetest public things that is happening in England.

The Listener, 25 October 1962

God and I

They do it every morning. They are dressed in a modified and decorated version of the outdoor clothes of the rich in Imperial Rome. Their utensils stand on stones that contain calcified fragments of those who are believed to have been killed because they refused to live a lie. They do it in colossal cathedrals, on kitchen tables, in chapels built on the cheap, at baroque altars in which an instant of religious drama has been frozen in stone and contrived light, in rooms over public houses that still smell of beer and occasionally, still, in upper rooms with the doors guarded. A man bends over a piece of unleavened bread and over a silver gilt cup with a little wine and water in it and he pronounces a formula more terrible than the sound of guns. '*Hoc est enim,*' it runs in part, '*corpus meum.*' And the majority of Christians believe that God himself is immediate and present, not in the way that he is everywhere anyway, but in the way that a man is there in the same room.

I have spent a large part of my life (less than I have spent sleeping or drinking or earning a living) recognising this conception on my knees. I have seen it done awkwardly on the back of a tank from a portable Mass kit. I have seen it done by friends and people I detested. I have attended it, sometimes with infinite boredom, sometimes with aesthetic impatience because it was badly done. But I cannot reject it. And all the glib anthropological explanations of this curious and, incidentally, beautiful 'sacrifice' leave me cold. I am, of course, a Catholic and a Catholic of a pretty conventional sort. I am neither an Evelyn Waugh nor a Graham Greene sort of Catholic. I can take or leave a dogma, set it on one side as irrelevant. I am in fact a pretty run-of-the-mill, second-class, civil service observant, intermittently loyal in a slightly football-team manner sort of Christian. The most I dare say is that I believe, I believe in God.

I came to this unsatisfactory state through no dark night of the soul. I was born a Catholic in England and I have never overtly rejected it. My father was a professional Catholic, a successful man who came up from the Irish diaspora and yet fell short of the glittering success he desired. He was an unhappy man who loved his family and yet could never express his love. Except when he was alive, I have felt no reason to rebel against him. I remain a Catholic and am in danger of becoming a professional too. To be quite honest, I believe in God because I was born to it. When I was small, my Sundays consisted of an early Mass with the expensive nurse who was paid primarily to keep us out of the way during the week. Then there came the solemn outing with my father to the highest, the most incense-laden, the most musically noisy and the longest Mass he could find. Then came, most awesome of all the ceremonies, Sunday luncheon, plain, long and laced with terrifying questions about the subject of the gospel of the day. And in the afternoon he would take us to a museum and top it off with vespers at the Oratory. Secretly – but I never let on – I liked this bit, because the choir was superb and the cantors used to swish their copes round their stools before they sat down in a gesture that was almost balletic. And they always did it in one.

I was educated in a school served by a Benedictine monastery and the many monks there I found happy and civilised, busy and socially useful. The organisation worked. There was also the extraordinary and austere beauty of the services. Anyone who swished a cope there would have got a flea in his ear from the Abbot. The monks used to field one of the best amateur rugby teams in Yorkshire. Above all they were sensible, moderate, friendly people, and when they were receiving guests told the only funny stories I have ever found tolerable for any length of time. To be a Christian there seemed the most natural thing in the world. Indeed, not to be a Christian seemed rather odd.

There is nothing odd about being brought up in such a Christian corridor. There are many other parallel corridors leading little boys to a predestined end. Some little boys, early or late, kick their way out of them – their walls are, after all, no thicker than a man's will. I have never felt the need to do this. Even at Oxford where one's certainties took a bad beating and one felt for a time like a turtle without a shell, there were priests and chaplains of such eminence and sophistication that the process of shedding one's shell became painless. The war was an interlude, served in the only regiment in the British Army that had Catholic chaplains, and anyway people do not lose their faith in wars. And after the war there was *The Observer* which, despite its former reputation for being a militantly anti-Catholic publication in a way that the *Guardian* is now, in fact was and is a pool of the most limpid tolerance. Indeed I became their domestic Catholic, useful on obscure doctrinal matters, not wholly reliable on Spain, a little cool about Pope John in the face of their enthusiasm, a slightly contemptible figure perhaps with my strange certainties and observances, but not for persecution or for censoring. For me they represent the fine flower of English tolerance; Catholics can be perfectly bloody and must seem at times intolerably dull.

This then is the story of my pedestrian spiritual Odyssey. It can help no one. It is so institutional, so conditioned and inevitable that it seems to include God only as the honorary chairman of the Patrick O'Donovan Education and Career Committee. But it leaves out the bread and the wine and the formula and the priesthood and the faith. Again it is all perfectly conventional. I kneel and I pray, though I find this hard. Such contact as I make is shot through with irrelevances like the beauty of a Palestrina Mass or a Salve Regina sung in a dark church without flamboyance. I take the Sacraments – they are my spiritual aspirins. I confess my sins and find it painful and embarrassing. In the country I attend a small, private, Guy Crouchback sort of chapel, where sometimes I have to present wine and water to the celebrant and read the Epistle and ring a horrid little bell at appropriate times, and I am torn between the vanity that I am making an elderly fool of myself and the idea that I am serving God.

Now it is true that the really noble soul can dispense with all this. The mystic who has known God can express his experience usually only in terms of poetry and sexual imagery. Such men can in the end dispense with ceremony, splendour and dogma and be alone with the alone. And, I think, it is this attitude to God that Malcolm Muggeridge is attempting to take. His description of the 'pursuing God,' his respect for monasticism, his loathing contempt for the world, these are the bare bones of mysticism which vary little whether they occur in a Christian, Moslem or Buddhist body. But that way is for the very few. For the rest there is the jolly, undemanding way of the open air and a vague pantheistic approach in which a man in an open-necked shirt feels good on top of Boar's Hill. A sight and a whiff of a withered rabbit, dead of myxomatosis in a hedgerow, should be enough to stop that lark.

There remains for the pedestrians the institutional approach. The fact of God is almost unbearable. He is the mathematics of infinity. It must have been much easier in the Middle Ages when the world was small, but now when we know a little of its population, of the crowding generations before us, of the demanding generations to come, of the universe that seems to have no limit, of the infinitely precious demand for identity of each single man, dead, alive or yet to be born, it is more difficult. The conception of God becomes so vast, so terrible, so unknowable that if I could really contain it I would collapse with awe and inadequacy each time I rang that silly little bell to signal His coming.

So perhaps I have reduced Him to manageable size. Or perhaps He has done it for people like me. I do not believe He is Old Beard on a cloud. I do not know that He exists in the same way that I know a Mr. Wilson is in Downing Street. Despite my indoctrination, I still have to make a conscious act of will to kneel and think before Him. Essentially He is, to me, unknowable. He dignifies my life as a journalist. He gives meaning to the deaths of my family and friends. Because I believe in Him I am surprised that I am not any nicer than the people I work with. But baldly and, in the end, inexplicably I believe He is there, that I owe Him devotion and that my life is richer for the experience that I am too embarrassed to pass on. This is an inadequate explanation, but then I was asked to be honest.

Nova, November 1967

Spiritual splendour

Many years ago when Dr. Heenan was living it up in Westminster, I was asked to take part in Charterhouse. I was told that I could write what I liked. I have fought the inclination to keep writing about myself and have occasionally failed. I have written often about hospitals, partly because I was inside one and partly because I was astonished by the spiritual splendour of nurses. I have also written about Christians, particularly about Catholics and, in a high-minded way expressed surprise that they are not obviously better than other people. I may have been wrong.

It is my wife who is now in hospital. She has been operated on a couple of weeks ago and is likely to be away for a good time to come. She is in a great teaching hospital in Southampton. It is big enough probably to contain the entire administrative apparatus of the Borough of Camden. She is on a floor where the beds are generously spaced and the care combines love and discipline and skill that still astonishes me. There are some fearful sights that now look merely human. The priest is as conscientious as the doctors. In addition to which, the lady who used to clean for us and cope when my wife could not, dropped dead a few days ago. She was a quiet, firm person of whom we were very fond and she coped without fuss.

Ours is a small town. I am alone in a house that seems to have got bigger. This time I have been astonished by the goodness of my neighbours. They bring me soup and figs from their greenhouses and brawn and lettuce. They do my typing at non-union hours. They cope with the dreariest bits of laundry and there is no patronage and no obvious pity and they concentrate their anxiety on my wife. They give me lifts to the hospital which is not close and make excuses to leave me alone in the small ward. The odd thing is that with only one or two exceptions they all seem to have connections of different sorts with a Christian church. Some are not very frequent churchgoers. Some have the memory of an act of transcendental kindness received from a church when they were in trouble. The Catholics are practical and she is prayed for each Sunday by name. I have learned that the comfortable world is full of suffering. Almost all these people have suffered and learned too and have not railed against God. They even leave me alone when the melancholy strikes like a malady.

There is nothing rare in my experience. I have merely got it wrong in the past. *The Catholic Herald, 23 October 1981*

A country funeral

I went to a country funeral the other day. The dead person was not landed gentry, no more in fact than a most hard working, useful and loved person. She was buried from the village church. This was not so much restored as rebuilt by the dreadful Sir Arthur Blomfield in 1898. There are bits of earlier churches scattered about it, including a Saxon crucifix outside the tower. It has a well used air and is a real facility in a real community.

The varying treatment of death is one of the symptoms of a society's attitude to God. The Catholics used to make a tremendous, cathartic triumph of it – at least for the great ones whose obsequies were for all the people. There were the glory of music, palls, vestments, mitres, candles (brown), guards and there were the prayers. The fascinating pagan *Dies Irae* and the tender almost naive leading away of the corpse in the *In Paradisum: 'Chorus Angelorum tecum suscipiat, et cum Lazaro quondam paupere aeternam habeas requiem.'* You cannot beat that for poignant comfort and revolutionary dignity. But we have watered down our splendours and there is a sort of terror now even about a requiem for a Pope.

For this funeral there was the rector in his surplice and black Anglican stole and the organist. The rector led in the coffin which was heaped with wreaths. 'I am the resurrection and the life ...' and the family came after, dozens of them in their best, the husband desolate, the church half full and it is a large church. The family settled into the peculiar crouch, not kneeling, but sitting and bending almost parallel with the ground.

I am not good at funerals. Some women weep at weddings. I choke up at funerals. I don't even have to have known the dead person. I can't finish the lines of all the hymns. I love graveyards and vaults where the coffins of the rich are filed in bins in the wall like enormous bottles of wine. But this putting away gives me not even a pleasurable melancholy. I was thinking about this even though I had been fond of the dead person. I decided that I really mourn the reality of death and most especially my own.

We sang the familiar hymns. The rector spoke and prayed with an utter clarity but never quite asking for her rest in Heaven, for eternity with God. And then the undertakers, still led by the rector, picked it up and carried it out into the cold afternoon. I noticed that just as at a marriage service the family formed into a precedence of relationships. We crunched down the gravel path, past hundreds of gravestones, some cared for, some growing nettles at their feet, some of the old country baroque ones arranged in rows, shoulder to shoulder so that the motor mower can get at the grass. The wind took and blew away the rector's voice. It is always so. They came to the empty grave where the reality of the naked heaps of raw earth were covered with imitation grass matting. The undertakers lowered the box with nautical gestures in silence. Wreaths had been laid out in the avenues on the grass, such meaningless things and yet, if they give comfort...

There was an enclosed silence around our little crowd with faces that were at once stricken and expressionless. There was a terrible beauty. We asserted our human dignity. A hard but not joyless life ended with a great, plain dignity. And then people drifted away, some pausing to look at the wreaths and their cards – as if they were trophies. People came out of the graveyard and did their shopping. Only the professionals stayed behind. The huge hired cars went away. The bell that had tolled for her in the old way was silent. And the coffin in the ground was left in the still unused part of the village depository.

The Catholic Herald, 30 October 1981

Postscript

ESTABLISHED 1791

THE OBSERVER

23 December 1981

Dear Mrs. O'Donovan,

I am writing to you to offer you sincere condolences, on behalf of many Observer colleagues and myself, on your loss. As I write, the news of Patrick's death has just reached the office and brought great sadness. We shall miss him very much. He wrote some of the best things 'The Observer' has ever published. Perhaps it is some small comfort in your ordeal to know that your personal loss is shared by so many.

He was much admired and respected, not only by those who had worked closely with him in David Astor's time: he was also a legend and an inspiration to the generation that followed. He gave dignity and nobility to the whole profession of journalism – we all felt that if a man of such towering talent could apply his gifts to our trade, then there must be something to be said for it. Patrick did immense good with his pen by opening up people's minds to the infinite riches and complexities of this life: he illuminated the world, lit it up to help others see more clearly. His compassion and his goodness showed in every line he wrote. All his fellow journalists marvelled at his professionalism – at the way he managed to disguise such learning, literary skill and sheer hard work in that elegant, simple, apparently effortless, inimitable style.

Yours sincerely,

Donald Trelford